Rewrite ~~GET WITH~~ THE PROGRAM

HOW TO STOP CONFORMING, START EXPLORING, AND FIND FULFILLMENT

ELI BOWMAN

Story BUILDERS PRESS

Rewrite the Program: How to Stop Conforming, Start Exploring, and Find Fulfillment

Copyright © 2026 Eli Bowman

Published by StoryBuilders Press

Edited by Korynne Adkins

Paperback: 979-8-89833-026-2

Hardcover: 979-8-89833-027-9

eBook: 979-8-89833-028-6

Audiobook: 979-8-89833-029-3

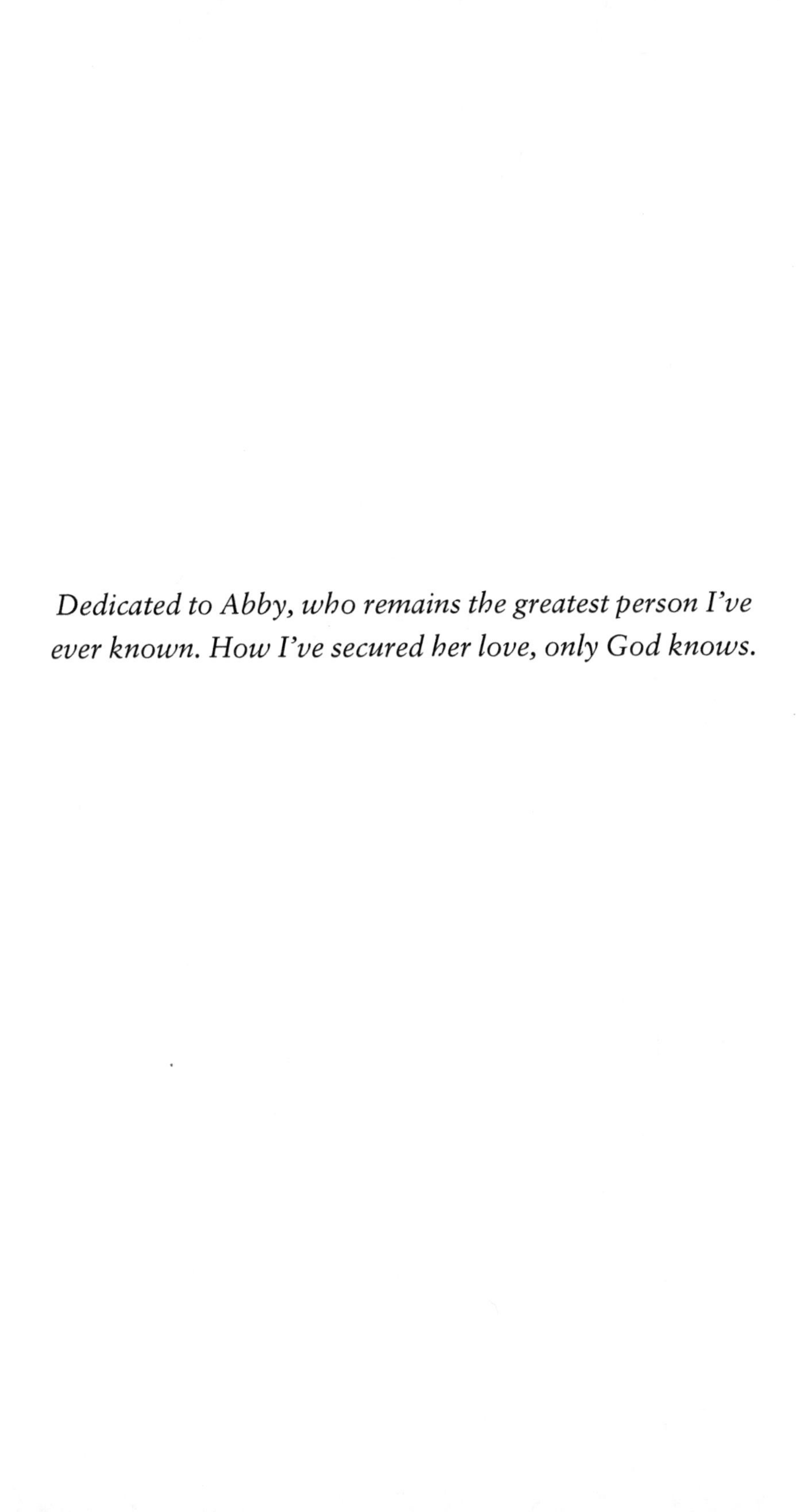

Dedicated to Abby, who remains the greatest person I've ever known. How I've secured her love, only God knows.

CONTENTS

AUTHOR'S NOTE

I was ten years old when I first witnessed real magic.

David Copperfield stood on stage at the Palace Theatre in Columbus, Ohio, and with nothing more than his words and focused intention, he did the impossible. In the span of half a second, he took what was essentially an empty stage and out of thin air placed on it a brand new Bugatti motorcycle with its engine running. A beautiful woman was sitting on top of it. One moment there was nothing. The next moment, a roaring machine and stunning performer materialized. The audience gasped. I sat transfixed, my young mind racing with a single, burning question: *How?*

That night I couldn't sleep. Not because I was trying to figure out the trick (though I was) but because something deeper had awakened in me. I had witnessed the impossible become possible through the power of focused intention and precise execution. I didn't know it then, but I had just received my first lesson in the power of the human mind.

Twenty-five years later I would discover that what I witnessed wasn't just an illusion; it was a demonstration of one of the most ancient and powerful principles known to humanity, a principle hidden in plain sight within a single, seemingly magical word: *abracadabra*.

Most people think abracadabra is just stage magic nonsense. But its etymology reveals something profound: ארבדכ ארבא (pronounced eh-vrah keh-dah-vrah), Hebrew for "I create as I speak." This wasn't a magician's catchphrase. It was an instruction manual for writing and installing your own mental programming.

You see, every single day, *you* are performing magic. With every thought you think, every word you speak (especially to yourself), and every story you tell about who you are and what's possible, you are literally conjuring your reality into existence. The problem is that most of us are unconscious magicians casting spells we never intended and creating lives we never wanted.

But here's the thing: Your unconscious mind is like a computer's operating system. It must run on programming of some kind. Just as your laptop can't function without software telling it how to process information, your unconscious mind requires code to operate. The question isn't whether you'll have programming running in the background of your mind (you absolutely will). The real question is this: Who wrote that code? And is it serving your highest good, or are you running outdated software that's keeping you stuck?

From the moment we're born, we are programmed—not by some conspiracy, but by well-meaning parents, teachers, society, and culture. These programs (unconscious patterns of thought and behavior) become the invisible scripts running our lives. Before we know it, we're living someone else's version of success, following someone else's definition of happiness, and pursuing someone else's dreams.

I know because I lived it. I followed every rule, checked every box, and achieved everything I was supposed to want—good college, stable career, nice house, growing family. From the outside, my life looked perfect. From the inside, I felt like I was suffocating. I had become a prisoner of my own programming, unconsciously creating a life that looked successful but felt hollow.

Then I hit rock bottom.

And in that darkness, I rediscovered the magic I'd witnessed as a ten-year-old boy. Not the sleight-of-hand kind but the real kind—the kind that happens when you learn to consciously rewrite the unconscious programs that are running your life.

Using principles rooted in neurolinguistic programming (NLP), neuroscience, and ancient wisdom traditions, I learned to identify the limiting beliefs and thought patterns that had been unconsciously creating my reality. More importantly, I learned to replace them with empowering programs aligned with my authentic purpose.

The results were nothing short of magical. After applying those principles, I built a portfolio of companies worth multiple seven figures. But more importantly, I learned to consciously create my reality. I transformed my marriage, my relationship with my children, my health, and my sense of purpose. I went from feeling like a victim of circumstance to becoming the conscious architect of my destiny.

The real magic, though, is that this isn't about me—this is about you.

Right now, as you read these words, programs are running in your unconscious mind. Some serve you, but many don't. Some were installed when you were five years old. Others were updated last week. All of them are creating your current reality, your relationships, your career satisfaction, your financial situation, your health, and your happiness.

The question is this: *Are you ready to become a conscious magician?*

In this book, you'll learn to identify the unconscious programs that are running your life, uninstall the ones that no longer serve you, and consciously install new ones aligned with your authentic purpose. You'll discover the framework to raise your self-awareness and literally rewrite your reality from the inside out.

This isn't positive thinking or wishful manifestation. It is practical neuroscience meets NLP meets inherent wisdom. This is learning to work with the same creative forces that David Copperfield demonstrated on that stage, even if they were for entertainment—the forces that govern how consciousness and unconsciousness shape our reality.

My own journey to governing my unconscious mind began on what should have been one of the most exciting days of my life.

Chapter 1

THE SEARCH FOR PURPOSE

I could feel the RV straining under the pressure of climbing the mountain. Cars, trucks, and semis zoomed past us as I slowed down to relieve the engine a little. I really wanted to make it to the next exit before pulling off.

My wife, Abby, sat in the passenger seat next to me, looking concerned. The RV had already overheated a few times that day, the first day of our travel life in early June 2018. All signs pointed to "this is a bad idea." I'm not one to give up though. We'd make this work—somehow.

"We need to pull over," Abby said, glancing back at our five kids.

"I know. I just want to get to the exit first," I responded, gritting my teeth.

"Why does this keep happening?" she asked.

"I have no clue. Otherwise I would've fixed it by now." I didn't like starting the trip out so tense, but I was getting frustrated. Even though this was a new-to-us RV, it was still in good shape. It shouldn't be breaking down at all, let alone multiple times in one day.

Just then I saw steam rising from the radiator area at the back of the RV.

"Ten more feet!" I yelled at the rig. We had pulled onto the exit ramp but couldn't stop so close to the turnoff. I lifted my foot from the gas pedal and glided to a spot in the grass on the side of the road.

Abby exhaled and unbuckled her seat belt.

"Time for another break, kids," Abby said as she made her way to the back.

We'd been driving all morning, heading south from our old life in Columbus, Ohio, to a campsite in Tennessee, but we were still several hours from our destination. I did what I'd been doing all day. I grabbed the small tool kit and the RV manual, and poked around the engine and radiator trying to diagnose why the engine kept overheating. But to be honest, I had no clue what I was looking for.

Google: Why is my RV engine overheating?

For the last few years, Abby had wanted to unplug from our life in Columbus. She'd dreamed about jumping into an RV, traveling, and teaching our kids about nature while hiking the woods of Appalachia or taking them to Thomas Jefferson's home rather than just reading about it in a book. And for years I had said no.

It wasn't part of the script.

It was too unpredictable.

I couldn't run a business from the road.

Then one day, everything broke. *I broke.* I finally understood that I was broken. The life I'd helped create no longer worked for me, and truly, it hadn't worked for our marriage for a long time.

It had been a gradual descent to my rock bottom, so much so that I couldn't see it until I slammed into granite. I had been stuck on the conveyor belt of life where one trouble begat the next. Abby and I married young at ages twenty-one and twenty-two because that's what we were supposed to do. I went to college to get a good job because that's what I was supposed to do. Then I started working insane hours at a job I hated because I was supposed to support my family. But because I was never home, Abby and I were growing apart. When our kids came along, she spent her days homeschooling and caring nonstop for our twins and triplets (yes, you read that right) while I worked twelve or more hours a day. And on and on it went. The punches kept coming.

The discontent grew. The despair grew. The feeling grew that I would never get out of this life I was starting to hate and yet had created for "good" reasons. I thought this was what it looked like and felt like to fulfill my purpose, or at least what I thought my purpose was. But I felt hollow inside—empty.

So the break had been a long time in the making. I should've seen it coming.

I think it started when I became more interested in politics a year or two before our trip. In the evenings after everyone went to bed, I researched and wrote political articles with a Libertarian bent. It felt good to be doing something that felt more important than my day job, something that would get people thinking or questioning the way we'd always done things. I also liked the idea of operating outside the typical system. I had been entrenched in the system, caught in its trappings my entire life—not just the political system but also the religion and society I'd been raised in. It was the just-so way of living and doing that I never quite fit into but went along with because I didn't know what else to do.

Asking questions felt like walking out of a dark cave and into the open with a bright blue sky above and nothing around—complete freedom. But the problem with questions is that once you start asking them about one part of life, they inevitably seep into other areas. *Why God? Why Mormonism? Why Abby? Why business and finance?* Before I knew it, all the pillars holding up my life began falling.

The next time Abby asked about the trip, her words finally reached me. I was ready for a massive change. I was desperate to try something new. I'd been running my own business for a while at that point, and honestly, I was losing interest in it without an idea of what would come next. Maybe this adventure would bring us back together in our marriage. Maybe I would finally have the time and space to figure out what I actually wanted.

Once I finally said yes in 2018, we got a gently used RV and were somehow ready to go within ninety days. Then we pulled out of our suburban driveway with a packed RV and what I thought would be a new lease on life. But the signs of impending disaster were there from that very first day as I stood on the side of the road next to the broken-down RV.

Believe me, these metaphors are not lost on me—at least not now.

No one had ever taught me how to drive a forty-one-foot diesel RV. I didn't know that you had to drive slowly uphill and take breaks. I was more intent on getting a vehicle to take my wife on the trip of her dreams than learning what that would entail. So here we were on our dream trip in a nightmare scenario.

As I searched the Internet for answers to my RV questions, I heard the kids becoming restless. It was June, and the day was already hot. Everyone was tired from the early start and sweaty from being in the RV with no air conditioning and hardly any wind to flow through the open windows. Abby came out of the vehicle and walked over to me. She peeked inside the panel where I was working and put her hand on my shoulder.

"How's it going?" she asked.

"It's going," I said.

"Do you think we'll be on the road soon?"

I straightened up and looked at her. "Depends on how soon I can get this thing to a mechanic," I said and laughed.

"Why are you laughing?"

"Because I don't know what else to do right now. I'm going to need some help with this."

After a little searching, I found a professional just an hour away, so we limped our way down to Farragut, Tennessee. We spent the next three days camping on-site at the mechanic's garage, waiting for them to fix our new home on wheels. Along with doing the repairs we needed, they gave us a little instruction on driving a 400-horsepower Cummins diesel engine. We were on the road again, hopefully on our way to living a charmed dream life.

For the next two or so years, my wife homeschooled our nine-year-old twins and six-year-old triplets while I drove us from one stop to another. During the day, we visited historical sites, state parks, and really anything we wanted to see. In the evenings, we pulled into a campsite or RV park and spent time around the campfire talking to each other, to new friends, and essentially just trying to enjoy time with one another.

I wasn't actively working during that time. We lived off the monthly residuals from my company. That gave Abby and me the time we'd been needing to reconnect, try to reconnect, or just connect. We didn't know each other anymore, even though we'd been together for fourteen years at that point. Being stuck together in an RV with no distractions began exposing the cracks in our marriage and frankly the cracks I'd been seeing in myself. And maybe that's what it was supposed to do all along.

As our marriage continued to deteriorate on the road, so did my business at home. Our monthly income was shrinking. Without my active participation in my company, it was crumbling. So in the evenings after we found a place to stay for the night, I started working again, trying to find new clients, make sales, rebuild something—anything—if we were going to keep traveling.

That's when the questions returned but with a new, twisted vengeance. *Why was my marriage falling apart when it wasn't part of the script? Am I potentially losing my family and my kids when that wasn't part of the script either? When did this all become so unpredictable? Why? Why am I still not happy?*

Why am I still unfulfilled? Why is this happening at all? Is any of this even fixable?

I can distinctly remember the night Abby and I decided to head home. We were camping in Virginia. The kids had gone to bed, and the two of us were still sitting outside around our dying campfire. It was a clear night, so we could see the stars. The wind was calm. The time was pretty late, and we'd stopped talking an hour earlier because there really wasn't much left to say. We'd said it and yelled it and cried it all over the last two years. The crickets were singing.

I looked over at Abby. She was sitting quietly, staring into the coals and thinking. I could feel my love and caring for her in my heart, but it was more like the last embers of a roaring fire, not the all-encompassing emotion I'd once felt for her. We'd invested so much in our life together and so much in each other. We weren't done yet. We couldn't be done yet. I put my head in my hands, willing myself to speak.

"Abby," I said, my face still buried in my hands.

"I know," she responded. Of course she'd felt it too. I was never in this alone, even if it had felt that way at times.

"Tell them tomorrow?" I asked, referring to the kids.

"Yeah. We'll tell them at breakfast that we're going home."

If we were going to make it, we had to go home. If we were going to have a fighting chance to fix what was broken between us—if I was going to have a chance to fix what I could feel broken in me—we had to get off this road because we were driving toward a total disaster.

Chapter 2

BREAK OUT OF THE PROGRAMMING

Have you ever played *Life*—you know, the children's board game with the colorful, winding path, the tiny plastic cars with the blue and pink peg people, and the mansion everyone wants or the shack you always seem to end up with?

The modern version I played as a kid in the '80s and '90s was actually based on a Milton Bradley game from 1860 called *Checkered Game of Life*.[1] While mine had squares that made me pay for summer school for the peg kids ($2,000 per child) or collect money for winning a photography prize ($2,000 total), the original was a simple checkered board with squares labeled things such as Fat Office, College, Industry, Bravery, Honor, Happiness, and Perseverance. Players of the 1860 game collected points for living a life according to the moral prescriptions of the day, whereas players of the 1980s version and beyond (that was reinvented in the 1960s based on Baby Boomer values and desires) were encouraged to amass the most wealth in order to win.[2] But whichever version you played, your choices and behavior were subtly influenced by the mechanics of the game—a perfect example of programming.

The life you're living right now is not a game, but you are still subtly influenced by the mechanics of your programming. There is a reason behind every decision you've made. Most of the time, that reason is an unconscious program that tells you something is right or wrong, desirable or undesirable. And most of the time, you didn't get to choose the programming you received; it just happened to you. Then, like the game of *Life*, you were funneled into a certain way of living, like the tiny cars on the colored squares, forced to spin the wheel and move the prescribed number of spaces each turn with almost no detours along the way. That way of living can many times produce a fine, just okay life. But when the mechanics governing your life—your programming—start to clash with the growing desires in your heart, it's impossible to know what to do next. You get stuck. Do you keep spinning and moving diligently forward, or do you pull off the path and ask who made the spinner? Who made the board? Who made the rules by which you're living your life?

If you've asked those kinds of questions, you're in good company. For me, this journey of exploration all started with one little word, one tiny dangerous and exciting question that broke the illusion of my life: *Why?*

WHO DESIGNED YOUR LIFE?

If you've picked up this book, I imagine you're feeling at least a little broken, stuck, or disconnected with yourself in some way. Something is out of alignment, but you're not sure what.

You might be asking yourself *why?* or you might be shying away from the *why*, knowing that the answer could break open in your life. Asking questions leads to seeking answers, and seeking answers can throw your whole world into chaos.

Most of the time things have to be broken before they can be fixed. We have to see how we're put together, what influenced us, and who created the script that is running our lives before we can choose how we want our life to be. I had to break my patterns before I could see the mechanics that were orchestrating them all.

I know it sounds bleak, but the RV trip wasn't completely dismantling. Yes, there were many times it did make things in my marriage and in myself worse—much worse—before it all got better. But there were also beautiful moments, usually centered on the children—times when Abby and I felt connected. Now, with the grace of hindsight, I can honestly say that trip eventually served its purpose. It helped us realign things in our marriage, and it helped me realign things in myself—just not in the time and way we'd imagined.

At least in the Western world, we have a pretty linear idea of life. We're born, go through school, get a job, find a spouse, settle down, have a family, and retire to someplace warm—and that's life. Doing those things and checking those boxes is supposed to make us happy and fulfill our purpose. That's the programming—the messaging and the habits that have been instilled in us our entire lives.

For most of us, though, it's more complicated than that. The *who, what, where, when, why,* and *how* make or break us, yet we often overlook those details. That's part of why we can't simply pick something such as arbitrarily choosing to be an accountant and then automatically be happy for the rest of our lives. What if you hate math and yet put yourself through the pain of a CPA program because that's what is expedient or what you've been told to do or conditioned to be your whole life—even if deep down you know it's not right for you?

That sounds crazy. Yet we do this and expect this all the time.

That's the power of programming.

However, programming is not all bad. Programs can serve us well at different points in our lives. Look at it like this: We will run on programming no matter what. Period. It's how our unconscious minds work. *It's good to brush your teeth, pay your bills, and not steal or lie.* That's all programming. The problems arise when your programming no longer serves you. If you are just going through the motions because you're supposed to go through the motions—getting married because you're supposed to get married, having kids because you're supposed to have kids, working a traditional nine-to-five because that's just what we all do—eventually you'll encounter some inner conflict born of misalignment of purpose, which will lead to myriad other manifestations of unhappiness, and eventually you will hit rock bottom. Everything will be sucked out of you. You will become a shell of yourself and who you're supposed to be.

When I started answering the *why* behind all the decisions that created my life, everything came down to the mental procedures or way of doing things instilled in me by the messages I'd received since childhood. Here are a few common ones circulating in our society:

- You have to go to school to get a good job.

- Men don't express their feelings to their wives.

- Husbands are the breadwinners of the family, and it has to be in a stable occupation, first choice being corporate.

- You have to get married.

- You have to at least go through the motions of whatever faith community you belong to, whether you actually know why or even whether you truly believe the messages.

Some of these may resonate with you, and some of them won't. What I've learned and know to be true is that drilling down on your why—pinpointing the motivation behind the choices you've made and the actions you take every day—is the first step in taking control of your life in order to align with your purpose.

Why must you investigate your *why*? Because when you understand your motivation and how you found yourself in this position, you can see through the subtle messaging that has steered you here. And when you can see it, like Neo waking up and seeing the matrix for what it was, you can change it. You will be able to uninstall the wrong programming that's driving your life, choose what programming (habits and thoughts patterns) you want to have, and tap into the *why* residing deep within you at the soul level. You will finally be able to connect with the reason you were born and the purpose you were meant to fulfill. In this beautiful place, a joyful day-to-day life can become common, where smiles rarely leave your face.

When I began this transformational process of uninstalling my programming—pinpointing the places where my life didn't seem to match the purpose written in my heart—honestly, it was terrifying. I felt like I was going against everything I'd been taught. I was afraid my mother would think I was ungrateful for the life she and my late father had given me and the values they had instilled in me. I worried if it would tear Abby and me farther apart. I was anxious about how it might radically change my parenting or my relationship with my kids. Yet what I found was that the people who loved me—Abby, my mother, my kids, my siblings—only wanted the best for me and for me to be happy and aligned with my purpose.

In fact, and this isn't rocket science, being a fulfilled person made me a better husband, father, son, and brother. And it will help you be the best version of yourself for you and your loved ones as well.

That's not to say you may not run into resistance from the people in your life. I've already mentioned how I was really the first line of resistance to my own change. Once you've overcome your own resistance, you'll find that when you begin to uproot programming that is as old as you are (or older), the people around you will begin to see a change in you. Some of those people, usually the ones who care most for you, will express unwavering support as you grow and evolve. Others will be less supportive, sometimes even covertly hoping you'll fail and fall back to your baseline. Those people see your progress as a threat to their perception of you, and it will remind them of the work they aren't doing for themselves. That sadly results in broken relationships and in most cases can't be avoided by those who progress quickly and significantly in their self-awareness. It's also not to say that it won't rock your foundations, because it will.

But uninstalling the programming of the world will allow you to tune in to your authentic purpose and align your life with that purpose. In other words, you'll be able to live the life only you can lead. And the world actually needs you to do that as much as you need to do it for yourself.

The other part of this is that it takes time and effort to pull back the veil on your life to find your center. It takes time to figure out what's misaligned in order to set everything as it should be. You may start the process and think you've found the answers only to realize later that you weren't quite done with the work. That is deeply entrenched stuff, so don't be hard on yourself if that's the case. I know; that's what happened to me.

# Checkpoint

Throughout the rest of this book, you'll hit checkpoints after each chapter. They are designed to create space for you to reflect on the information and stories in the chapters as well as in your own life. As I said earlier, there's a reason you picked up this book. I want to help you begin to process what that reason might be and pinpoint the areas of your life that don't feel aligned.

I truly believe that everyone was born with something in their hearts that needs to be—and should be—expressed. But most of the time, for whatever reason, we either don't have the opportunity to express it or choose not to do so, which frankly is a tragedy. However, we don't have to stay mired in the wrong programs that are running our lives. We can fix what is broken, change what needs to be changed, and live aligned with our purpose.

So before you jump into Chapter 3, think about, journal about, or talk with someone about the following questions:

- What dynamics in your early childhood and young adulthood led you to where you currently are in life?

    - Were you inspired to follow in someone's footsteps?

    - Did you receive advice about what you should do when you grew up?

- Were you pushed or pulled in some way to do what you're doing and how you're doing it?

- Were you free to follow whatever path you chose?

✎ Have you started noticing certain thought patterns or emotions that arise in response to certain situations?

Chapter 3

THE WINDING ROAD TO PURPOSE

While the RV trip in 2018 was a wake-up call for most of the things in my life that needed attention, I'd actually started down the path of finding my true purpose back in 2009.

After Abby and I were married in 2004, I landed a job I was really good at in corporate finance. I worked long days for big paychecks and praise from my family for doing such a good job and being a good provider. I was winning the Game of Life. I worked in that world for years to support our growing family, even though in my heart I knew it wasn't the right *kind* of work.

Then in 2009, I was laid off. That could have been a natural time to explore or begin questioning why I was working in finance and banking (because I hated it), but I was mired in the programming. I didn't know any other way of living or being. And I had a family to support. Needing a job—any job—I continued to operate on autopilot, becoming more and more misaligned and doing work I hated for the next three years.

(That makes it sound like I didn't start my journey until 2012, but it really was 2009. All will be revealed.)

In 2012, at age thirty, I hit my first pivot point. It had been another tough day in a string of tough years. I would leave the house while the kids were eating breakfast, come home in the evening to eat dinner as a family, and help put the kids to bed. Then I'd give Abby a kiss on the cheek and drive all the way back to the office to work until midnight, only to return home to a house full of sleeping people. Rinse and repeat. It was a never-ending story of soul-crushing hustle. I'd done that kind of work since my college internship, and I thought I was past the acceptable career-exploration phase of my life. I had an idea that maybe I should start my own business, but it seemed too unstable, and I needed stability to care for my family. So I dismissed the whole thing—until the feelings became too profound to ignore.

On one of those countless nights, I lay in bed staring at the ceiling. I often had trouble falling asleep and couldn't stop the typical barrage of questions from swirling around in my head. *Why am I trading all my time with my family for a job I don't even like? Why don't I just do something different? Why can't I let myself change things? What am I really afraid of?*

There had to be a reason why I was doing what I was doing, right? There had to be a reason why I was making myself so miserable. *Would I ever tell my kids to do work they hated and encourage them to go live a miserable life?* No. So why was I asking it of myself? The longer I worked those finance jobs, the more I felt a sense of professional aimlessness that was seeping into my personal life and creating a black hole at the center of my being that would continue to grow if I didn't do something to stop it.

After another fitful night of sleep, I called my sister.

"Hey, I really feel like I need to do my own thing and start a business," I told her.

Then my programming kicked in, and right away, I started giving her all the reasons I shouldn't—we have five kids, we need a stable paycheck, we need insurance and retirement plans, we have a mortgage, and on and on. I think I ended with this: "It's too late for me to take these risks. My life has already started."

But instead of agreeing with me, she asked if I really felt that way. Did I feel like becoming an entrepreneur was the right thing to do?

I found myself saying, "With my whole soul I feel like this is what I'm supposed to do."

"Do you believe it's what God wants you to do?" she asked.

"Yes, I believe it's what God wants me to do."

"Then why are you afraid?"

I really want to make sure it's clear here how instantly and wildly things changed inside my mind and heart when she asked me that last question. The way I saw all my self-imposed resistance exposed in a moment—exposed with yet another *why*—was glorious. So much of the fear that had gripped my soul over this decision simply melted away when I knew that my higher purpose was aligned with becoming an entrepreneur.

It seemed insane that I couldn't or hadn't seen the answer before. It was so simple. I felt like God was with me on this, so why was I so afraid? It was simple yet so elusive due to my programming.

Another way to look at it is that I'd only been considering the *limitations* and not the *possibilities*—the limitations that came from my programming, not the possibilities found in my purpose.

Soon after that conversation, I started my first successful company.

The next ten-ish years were full of highs and lows as I founded and ran a handful of companies. I was learning my strengths and weaknesses, discovering what was aligned with my purpose and what wasn't, and trying new things. Everything was good for quite a while, but slowly my view of the businesses shifted. Instead of finding new ways to solve problems, I was focusing on ways to make money. I was falling back into old mental patterns of amassing financial wealth instead of amassing well-being for me and my family. I was full of discontent because I just didn't know why I couldn't seem to stop doing the same things over and over.

Perhaps the bigger problem was that no one could see the disconnect I felt; they just saw a young man working hard, making money, and taking care of his family. Not that these weren't and aren't noble pursuits—they're just not the *only* noble pursuits.

SEEKING SOMETHING MORE

As a child, I was an atypical learner. I had both ADHD and Tourette syndrome, yet I taught myself to read when I was three years old. Looking back, I know I was bright and intelligent, but I didn't present in the neurotypical way that school administrators in the '80s and '90s wanted to see. They didn't know what to do with me. So I struggled.

I will always remember sitting in a room with a tutor when another tutor came in to speak with the first one. They stood by the door while they talked, but I could still hear them. The first tutor called me "dumb." I knew I wasn't, yet what alarmed me the most was that the teachers in my life *thought* I was dumb, which began to change how I saw myself. I began to believe them.

During that time, my parents did what they could to help me, but what made the most difference was their belief in me. It gave me hope.

If my mother said this once, she said it a hundred times: "Eli, you can and will accomplish great things. You can do and be anything you want. You are here on earth to do something very special." Despite what other adults in my life thought, I operated under this understanding that I could and *would* do something great.

While this thought bolstered me as a child, it also tore me apart as an adult. I thought about it throughout all my misery. It became the idea against which I measured every part of myself.

Is what I'm doing with my career great?

No.

Is it what I want to do?

No.

Am I happy?

No.

Am I happy in my marriage?

No.

Am I happy at work?

No.

Am I happy with my faith?

No.

Why?

When I started questioning everything, the guilt and shame kicked in. Was I really so ungrateful for everything? Could I be happy in the areas of my life that mattered most and still be able to change it in others? I wrestled with those questions for a long time.

This may all sound selfish. But at the heart, it's about living a life of alignment in purpose, doing work that feels meaningful inside and out, and as a result being fulfilled and reaching our highest potential. As my mother said for me, I will say for you: *I believe you are here to do something great, something very special.* Maybe it's finding the cure for cancer or bringing about world peace or feeding every hungry person in America. Or maybe it's raising great and awesome kids with strong character and values who change the world. Whatever it might be, that's what I'll help you find because that's what I've finally found.

Looking back, I see that first layoff in 2009 as a gift that pushed me out of the wrong job. I had stayed there too many years, pushing off living my true purpose. Since I didn't take the opportunity for the first course correction, when I was presented with another situation in 2012, I finally listened to the urgency in my heart to start my own business. And yet being an entrepreneur only felt like my purpose until I found myself being solely driven by money—a feeling I could ignore while we traveled until there was another crisis in my life and in my work.

When we arrived home from the RV trip, I not only tried to breathe new life into my dying business but also started a brand-new company doing something I'd never done before. While I'd had some small successes in the past nine or so years, this time the business really took off, and I began to have the success I'd always wanted. And again, I felt like I was living my purpose . . . until I wasn't, again. I had slipped back into my old patterns. How? Because the programming ran *that* deep. No matter what I did, I couldn't seem to break my ingrained habits—self-sabotage, poor diet, little exercise, no reading, being dishonest with myself about my life, turning to vices to numb my pain, and a few others.

The worst of the worst of everything for me came in 2023. That spring, I hit rock bottom emotionally, physically, and spiritually. I hit rock bottom in my marriage, in my self-esteem, and you name it. Somehow, that period was worse than the RV trip in every way. The problems in my marriage grew to the point where I moved out and was living with a friend. My self-esteem was so low that I had suicidal thoughts.

By summer and after much work, things between me and Abby had healed enough for me to move back in with my family. But we didn't stop there—we both continued to do the work to save our marriage. After that, things got better fast. I started working out and eating better to get in shape. My largest company (I had a few at the time) was going like gangbusters. The kids were thriving. I was coming to peaceful terms with my spirituality. Everything felt right again. I was getting closer and closer to alignment . . . or so it seemed.

Then my biggest customer pulled the rug out from under my company. I felt like I was losing control.

But I was glad.

I was happy to watch it burn because it felt like losing my most lucrative business was getting my life back, if that makes any sense. Fast forward a couple months, and I found myself standing in a room filled with people full of purpose, which had been all I wanted. The twist? I thought I was at a weekend retreat to explore my purpose when really it was a week-long training certification for neuro-linguistic programming.

As confused as I initially was about being there, it was exactly what I had needed all along.

Checkpoint

Not all programming in our lives is negative or wrong for us. As the saying goes, there is a season for everything. And it's okay to look back on those seasons with joy. That's part of what keeps us in our programming.

But right now, I want you to think back to times when you seemed to be operating from your own internal, natural motivation—not from your programming. Take a moment to get into that headspace. When you're ready, consider these questions:

- What activities did you enjoy as a kid *just because*? Don't think about whether they were "useful" or "productive." Think about the times you could get lost in what you were doing, when you felt the most alive and excited. What were they?

- Taking it deeper, what specifically did you like about them? Were there certain aspects that really captured you?

- Are you using any of those skills, or do you get to do similar activities now?

  - If not, why? How much better would your life be if you were engaged in those activities?

Understanding this brief period of contentment provides valuable insight into your authentic being before social adaptation—that's where our authentic purpose lives. As we get more in tune with what we want and need in our lives as adults, we naturally start looking for ways to realign with that inherent purpose in order to thrive. There are more mature forms of this childhood fulfillment that you can recapture in a conscious way.

Tapping back into those early memories, did you ever have a desire to do or be a specific thing when you grew up, for no other reason than it spoke to you? In other words, you just felt pulled toward it for a reason you didn't understand.

That's what I want you to explore as we continue. What do you feel like you are or were being called to do before the world taught you otherwise? What work speaks to you?

Chapter 4

REALIGNING WITH YOUR PURPOSE

"Where are we?" I asked my friend.

The event organizers had just given their opening remarks to kick off the week-long neuro-linguistic programming certification training, and everyone around me was getting ready to move into the exercise room for some starter activities. I'd only heard about the event a few days earlier. Thinking it was an inspirational retreat (based on my friend's description), I registered without much investigation and bought a ticket to fly from Ohio to Dallas. Now, here I was, looking through the scheduled workshops and exercises with names like "Releasing Negative Emotions" and "Reframing."

What have I gotten myself into? I thought.

Everyone else knew why they were there. They were either working to become certified NLP practitioners or they were already certified NLP practitioners who wanted to add a few extra arrows to their quivers. And then there was me, a person searching for answers about my life and purpose.

"It's a neuro-linguistic programming certification," my friend answered, as if he'd explained it in detail already.

"A what? I thought this was a retreat," I replied. "I'm just looking for something to pump me up and get me feeling good, confident, and happy—just a get-right-in-my-mind kind of thing."

"Oh, this'll be inspirational and reset your mind. Trust me," he insisted. With that, he dragged me into my first NLP exercise.

For the next five days, for ten to twelve hours at a stretch, I was held captive, learning everything there is about NLP and how to be an NLP practitioner. I say "captive" as a joke because really, I could have left at any point. But I was hooked. Everything I heard answered one of the lingering questions I'd had about my life. Being immersed in that world allowed me to be fully present for the first time in a long time. It was like neurons were going off constantly. New synaptic connections were being made; new realizations, new understandings, and new learnings were constantly taking place. With every workshop and seminar I was finally understanding how human beings think, how *I* thought, and how we all have the power to rewrite those connections—change our programming—into anything we want. We always have the power to realign with our purpose.

It was a very pivotal moment.

By the end of the week, not only had I played the role of practitioner but also that of client, undergoing the process of NLP therapy. I began the process of releasing a lot of my negative, ingrained habits such as the pressure to please others no matter the cost to me , the things that had kept me feeling misaligned for so long. I also started breaking up patterns in my life that had been holding me back from discovering and living my purpose. I began to give myself permission to live a life authentic to my wants and desires. Finally, I let go of old emotions tied to past events and people who kept my body locked in a particular state of being, one that kept me from moving forward. I left there very empowered, just as my friend had said I would. I finally had a path forward.

And that's what I want to do for you. I want to help you realign your thoughts and patterns so you can start to live your life of purpose and service.

THE ABCs OF NLP

From the moment we're born, we're like sponges. We soak up many things:

- How our parents and family members act

- What teachers tell us is "right" or "wrong"

- What our friends think is "cool" or "uncool"

- The way our institutions promote or condemn certain behaviors

- What our culture says we "should" do

- Early experiences that teach us about life

All this becomes a recipe book in our minds that tells us how to think, feel, and behave. While these "recipes" often feel set in stone (maybe you've tried to change them before and failed), they're actually not. We can change these mental recipes using NLP techniques.

If you're not already familiar with NLP, it is the study of these recipes, the unconscious decision-making that drives our thoughts and behaviors. It helps us pinpoint those recipes that have been instilled in us since birth and shows us how to "uninstall" them, allowing us to choose our actions, our paths, our responses, and more. It creates the space we need to reconnect with our authentic selves. Think of it like updating old software on your computer. Through NLP, you can do the following:

- Identify thoughts and beliefs that hold you back

- Figure out where they came from

- Replace them with better ones

- Practice new ways of thinking until they become natural

NLP can also explain why we don't chase our dreams even when we really want to. Some of us get comfortable with what's familiar, even if it doesn't feel aligned with who we really are. Our brain likes to stay safe and comfortable rather than take risks. But when we stay in that safe and comfortable routine day in and day out, we're reinforcing the patterns and habits that are holding us back; they become like deep grooves in our brains. Others are just as scared of success as they are of failure. And the rest of us might not even realize what's holding us back, so we can't do anything about it, even if we want to.

By the time I started learning about NLP, I had already tried and failed to address my misalignment issues through traditional talk therapy. I even had two therapists at one point. But typical talk therapy was slow and, for me, ineffective.

So out of desperation I turned to neuroscience and biohacking approaches—things that had a direct impact on the brain such as walking in the morning to get sunlight into my eyes and reset my circadian rhythms, undergoing red light therapy, sitting in saunas, and experiencing cryotherapy. To some extent they worked well. They helped me feel better about myself.

What they didn't do, though, was answer all my glaring questions about life such as *How did I get so far down into this pit of despair and desperation?* Not until I was introduced to NLP did the light bulb go off and all the missing puzzle pieces fall into place. But when they did, I finally had a way to understand and even explain how I had gotten to that point. And that's what I needed so badly.

You see, your mind is like a garden. You can pull out weeds (outdated or now-unhelpful habits and thought patterns) and plant flowers (ways of being that serve us now). But what most of us fail to realize is that *we* are the gardeners. *We* are the landscapers. We can choose what to weed and what to plant and where.

While we have this power, change happens one thought and one action at a time, just as you would pull one weed at a time or plant one bulb at a time in a literal garden. Small daily choices lead to big life changes, but it can take a season of weeding and planting before you see the flower. You have the power to rewrite any story that doesn't serve you. Move that apple tree if you don't like it in the corner. Your future isn't limited by your past. You can make your garden anything you want it to be. Put in a koi pond if you want.

The key is understanding that while our early programming *shaped* us, it doesn't have to *define* us, nor should it. We can choose new ways of thinking and being that align with who we want to become or who we truly are. Instead of "I'm too old to start something new," you learn to think, "My experience gives me an advantage." Or you replace "I'm not good enough" with "I'm learning and growing every day." You can turn "What if I fail?" into "What if I succeed?"

Humor me for a second here, but this transformational process makes me think of the animated TV series *Dragon Ball Z*. You don't need to know the show to understand this illustration. Right before the characters change into their ultra-powerful, *Super Saiyan* forms, there's a moment when they almost collapse in on themselves in a sense. They're pulling in energy from all around them. When they've absorbed as much as they can and their transformation is complete, the power explodes outward, sometimes with their arms thrown wide, the new power radiating out from their bodies.

When you're at rock bottom, it's like you've collapsed in on yourself. You're absorbing energy from all around you. While you may look the same on the outside, the transformation happening on the inside is revolutionary. It's life-changing. It's soul-changing. And it shakes everything. That's why it hurts. But then we just explode with unbelievable power.

There's hope at the end of this journey. You may be collapsing in on yourself right now. It may hurt so bad that you can't remember what life was like before, but there's an internal transformation taking place. If that's where you are, then trust me; you're about to explode into your ultra-powerful form.

THE TWIST: REALIGNING WITH YOUR SOUL'S CALLING

Throughout the rest of this book, I will show you how NLP explains what is happening for you right now and why you feel misaligned. You'll want to begin the process of identifying your negative programming, uninstalling it, and then installing the programming that will help you live the life you want. I say "begin the process" because it's just that—something you may have to do over and over as you find hidden programs in your psyche that are holding you back.

Along with this understanding, you'll keep using the Checkpoints between chapters to identify your purpose and help you determine what you need to do in order to align with it. At the beginning, that can seem daunting. But most of us know when something isn't right, and with a little work, we can figure out why it's wrong. Once you know the *why* (it always goes back to *why*), what you need to do to get from here to there becomes clear.

NLP really kickstarted the self-discovery process for me. Through the NLP techniques of understanding my programming, eliminating the cycle of dissatisfaction from my life, dismantling the limiting beliefs holding me hostage, and shifting my perspective, I was able to rediscover my authentic purpose. I was able to look at my life and my heart with a clear perspective to find the calling that had been written into my DNA.

If you're deep in the programming, this soul-calling has been buried. Maybe you catch a glimpse of it from time to time, but you're unable to act on it. So first, you have to clear away everything that's in your way. Only then can your authentic purpose come to light to give you direction.

When I talk about purpose, I'm building upon the Japanese idea of *ikigai*, which is about finding your calling.

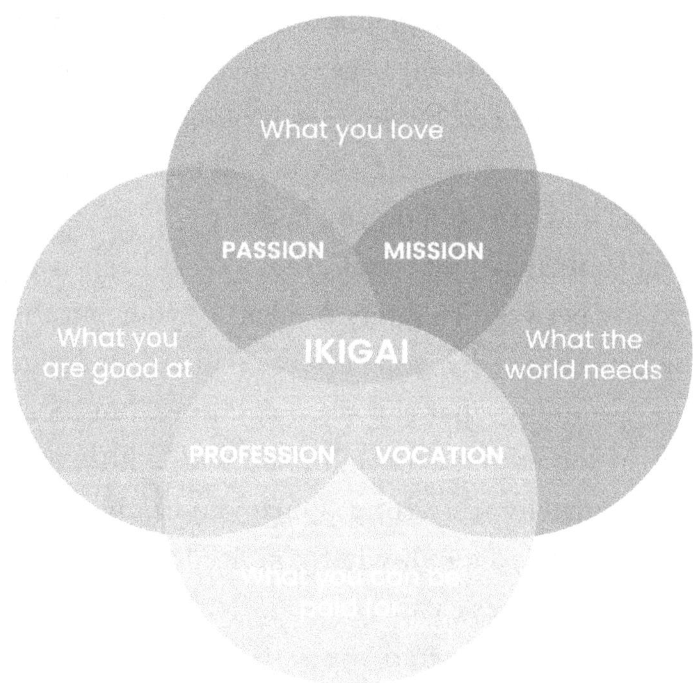

As you can see in the diagram above, your ikigai is the intersection of what you love, what the world needs, what you can be paid for, and what you're good at. If we were just keeping to the concept of ikigai, that is where we would stop—the end. You would live your life of ikigai just as it is.

But what I'm proposing doesn't stop there. It goes bigger. And bigger. And bigger.

Even right now, you may already have some satisfaction in some of these areas. Maybe you already know your mission, or maybe you like your job. Maybe your family life is perfect. But there's clearly something that's out of alignment because you've picked up this book. That's where my Path of Purpose comes in.

I have always liked how approachable the ikigai framework is. It's very easy to understand. But it can be difficult and at times impossible to apply in life—*at least in Western society.* The reason it can be impossible to implement is because of the programming that's running our lives. As you'll see, the Path of Purpose combines NLP work with ikigai and pushes the boundaries. You must first uninstall the programs imposed upon you in order to rediscover your purpose.

Below is the Path of Purpose. There are four quadrants to this journey: Conveyor Belt, Deconstruction, Enlightenment, and Impact. To walk the path, you must move clockwise through each of the four quadrants or stages in order to find and fulfill your authentic calling—Conveyor Belt to Deconstruction to Enlightenment to Impact.

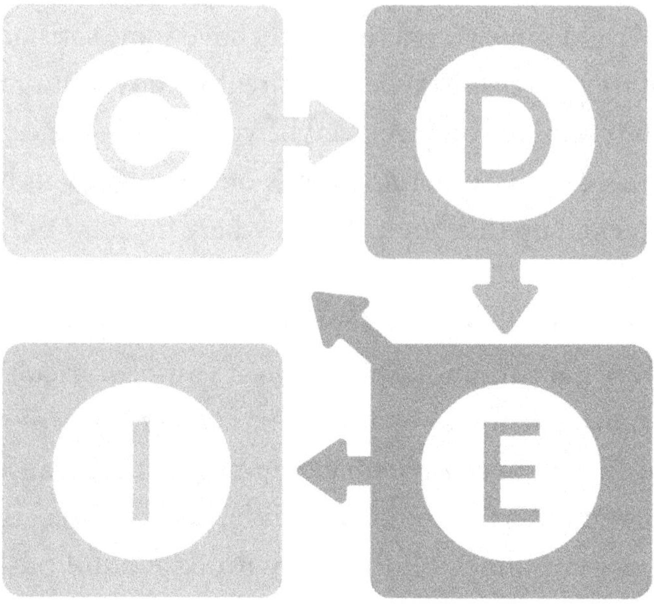

Further, within each quadrant, you progress through a series of four subquadrants that prepare you for entering the next main quadrant. Some people have naturally moved through this process and ended up living their purpose without much thought as to the mechanics. But for the rest of us, and I would argue the majority of us, we get trapped in certain stages and don't know how to move on. The programming is so strong that we don't know that it exists or how to dismantle it to realign with our purpose. That's why I've written this book.

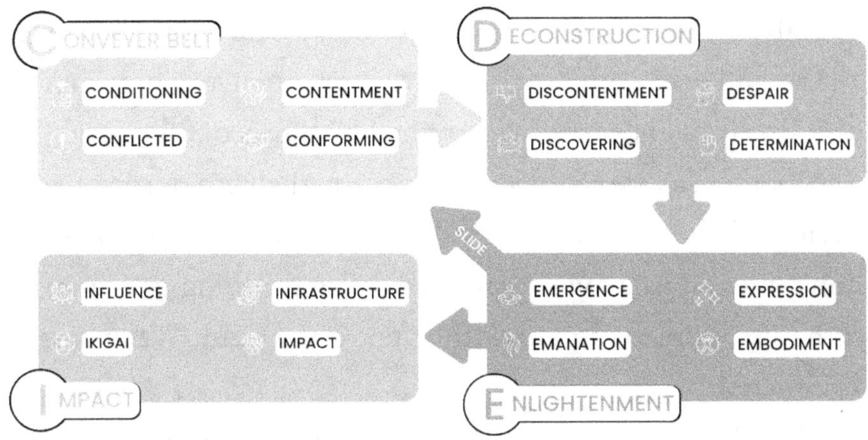

UNDERSTANDING THE PATH OF PURPOSE

Like life, the Path of Purpose is a winding road. There are many places to stop and linger or places where you might decide to turn around. Throughout the rest of the book, we'll dive deeper into the Path of Purpose and fully immerse ourselves in every step of each quadrant, but I want to give you a preview of where we're headed. So we'll begin where our lives start—in the first quadrant, Conveyor Belt.

We are born into the world as baby blank slates. Very quickly, though, through living life and just being in the world, Conditioning occurs. It's normal. It happens everywhere and in every culture. We become programmed by those around us, and we start living our lives on autopilot.

For a while, it's all great. We're Content. We've done the things we're supposed to have done, and so we've Conformed to the life we were supposed to live—an external idea of who and how others want us to be, not who our heart or soul intends for us to be. Keep in mind, though, that we've chosen all this and been complicit in the creation, no matter how much of it was influenced and determined by our programming.

But then, as we get older and more settled into our lives, we begin to realize that maybe we don't like what's happening. We don't like our jobs. We've stopped doing the things that make us happy. Something feels off or not quite right. We become Conflicted.

That's when we move into the second quadrant: Deconstruction. The conflict in our hearts and minds starts breaking the illusion of the life we've created. Yes, even though the programming is strong, we are all still complicit in creating the wrong life. We become Disenchanted with it. We begin reviewing the pillars and systems holding up our lives and see them differently, recognizing what they truly are—external programs installed without our initial consent. More often than not, finally seeing the false scaffolding of our lives and beginning to ask the questions we've been terrified to ask throws us into deep Despair. But we must dismantle the programming if we're ever going to find what's authentic and true in our lives. (I described being in this stage in Chapter 1 and working through it in Chapter 2.)

Once we start asking questions, we become Determined to figure it all out. We start actively Discovering possibilities to pursue something that makes us happy or something we believe is meaningful or purposeful. And there is fulfillment to be found here; it's a spectrum. But it's not the end.

From here, we shift into the third quadrant: Enlightenment. As we're discovering, those things we naturally love begin to Emerge, and we make space for them to take root once more in our lives. There's a big difference between discovery and emergence because people like the idea of doing what they love, but there's something holding them back from jumping all in, from allowing themselves to be as they are. I think about it like maybe you're an accountant, but you've always loved photography. As you worked through the Deconstruction Quadrant, you remember your love of photography, so you buy a camera and start shooting photos on the weekends. Maybe you're getting paid or maybe it's just for fun. Either way, you're opening up to this emergence of something that feels like an extension of you.

As you begin to dive more deeply into that world, you show others what you're doing. Maybe you exhibit photos at a local coffee shop, or maybe you photograph your friend's family. That's Emergence. The progression is quite natural and lights you up. You start deliberating about how to act in a way that aligns with your interest.

At this point, you might try to start a side hustle or business to lean even more into your interest. That is Expression. After that, you might quit your accounting job and go all in, which is Embodiment. You're feeling aligned that this is the right thing right now.

At this point, we radiate a new kind of energy that draws people to us—Emanation—which positions us for more success.

However, when we reach Embodiment, we face a choice. You could stop there and live a completely fulfilling, ikigai-aligned life. Or you could go bigger and make real and lasting change in the world through serving others. The latter takes a different kind of commitment and risk. It could also take a hard and deep change to your day-to-day life to scale it. But this is also where the most amazing things happen.

If we make the choice of going all in, no matter the challenges, that's when we move into the final quadrant: Impact. By this point, we've reached our ikigai—we've brought together what we're good at with what we love with what we can get paid for with what the world needs—and we see the people in our lives taking notice and making positive changes in their own lives as a result. When this happens, it inspires a desire to help more people make the change they need to live their best, most aligned lives. So we take steps to scale what we're living and doing through expanding our Influence on others on purpose. We dig into building social media followings or in-person groups in our towns and cities. We create courses, write books, or take steps to get the word out. To do that well, we have to also create the Infrastructure needed to support all this action in the long term. In turn, this grows our Impact. It becomes immeasurable because the people we've helped directly are now helping others in their own lives in ways we can't see or know. As we live and grow in all this, we arrive at a global impact of Ikigai.

Go back to the photography example. You've done it, you love it, the world needs it, and you're getting paid to do it. So you ask yourself, *How can I make this more fulfilling?* Maybe you can write a book on photography, start a podcast, teach others how to do it, volunteer somewhere, or document an event for an organization. You're spreading the gospel of photography. You're making it about more than yourself. You might start an organization that gets cameras and training into the hands of people who can't afford those things on their own. In that way, they're able to bring their photos and experiences to people around the world who might not know their story. Maybe that teaches them the skills they need to start their own small businesses that lift up their families. Maybe it inspires others to chase their own non-photography-related purposes, and so on. This global impact of ikigai is operating from the highest joy and purpose. It is the peak of what we can experience when we wake up every day.

There are two more points about the Path of Purpose. First, there's no set amount of time it takes people to move through the subquadrants of each quadrant or to move from one quadrant to the next. You may spend years on the Conveyor Belt and Deconstruction before getting to Enlightenment. In fact, you may stay in Enlightenment because everything is good enough. But once you fall into good enough, you may slide back into the Conveyor Belt, specifically into conforming, although that is now a Conveyor Belt of your own conscious making. At some point, you may cycle back through Deconstruction and Enlightenment and come upon something new. Maybe that moves you to Impact. Or maybe you slide back onto the Conveyor Belt again.

Second, when we're in Conveyor Belt and Deconstruction, we're in a passive state of living, or nonliving. Things are happening to us, and we're going along with them. We're not engaged in our lives. However, as we move from Discovery in

Deconstruction to Emerging in Enlightenment, we're taking the reins. We're making the decisions. We're taking action. We're making change happen. In other words, we're in an active state of living. We're becoming fully alive.

The point of this book is to help you move through the entire process to Impact. But it's always your choice about how much time you want and need to spend in any given quadrant. You can read and reread any chapter of this book. Do the exercises over and over again. Set up an appointment with a coach or come to one of my events to work through whatever quadrant or subquadrant you might find yourself stuck in. It's a journey. It's the Path of Purpose. And now that you know about it, you have the power to walk it however you need in order to create a life aligned with your authentic purpose.

In Chapters 5 through 9, we will cover the five-step process to take back control of your life and work through the Path of Purpose.

- Chapter 5 is all about awareness and recognizing your mental and emotional conditioning—programs. I think of it as rewriting your mind's story. You want to understand what your current story is and what messages you heard growing up. You'll want to find out what you tell yourself is possible, and consider how your past shapes your present. In doing so, you'll work through the subquadrants of the Conveyor Belt and begin to dip into the subquadrants of Deconstruction.

- Chapter 6 will take you through the Deconstruction Quadrant, identifying and processing the negative emotions you'll feel once you've identified your programming. When you've come to terms with that programming, you'll become set on rediscovering your purpose and realigning with it. You'll find yourself naturally releasing what's holding you back in order to create the space for new growth, purpose, and fulfillment.

✎ Chapter 7 is all about the Enlightenment Quadrant, fully stepping into whatever brings you joy and fulfillment. That is where you first encounter feelings of ikigai and where you may choose to stay. But I would challenge you to go farther than you ever imagined possible and move into the fourth and final quadrant.

✎ Chapter 8 will help you shift your perspective in not just living your ikigai but using it to improve the lives of others directly and indirectly on a global scale through growing your Impact—the fourth quadrant. This is truly where fulfillment occurs. I don't believe we can live our purpose unless what we're doing is in some way serving others. Our lives and work don't happen in a vacuum, and I believe you were given certain skills for a reason. So whatever you do, do it as big as you can, and inspire and help as many people as possible along the way.

My hope is that by the time you reach Chapter 9, you have started making changes in your life to live more aligned with your authentic self and purpose. I know it's not easy to ask yourself, *Why this life? Why these choices?* But if you feel restless, if you feel like you're living someone else's life, if you've hit rock bottom and don't know how to get back to happiness, start with the question and see where the path leads you. Just as my parents told me, I'm telling you, *You can and will accomplish great things. You can do and be anything you want. You are here on earth to do something very special.*

So now, let's dive into the deeply ingrained patterns of programming.

Checkpoint

Something is wrong or at least doesn't feel right. It seems like you settled for a life you didn't intentionally build; it just kind of happened, and you went with it. That's not a judgment, trust me. That's simply the story of most people. *Most* of us go along with the flow because we don't realize that we can choose something different, or we don't want to create conflict by choosing a path that others don't understand.

And yet . . .

And yet now you're coming to terms with the errors of that thinking. Feeling misaligned in one or more areas of your life eventually spills over into other areas of your life. Think about the game *Jenga*. When it starts, the tower of blocks is strong and aligned well from top to bottom. Everything is in its place. But as the game progresses, pieces are pulled out, which inevitably knock into other pieces, pushing them slightly out of alignment. And after a few rounds, the tower becomes wonky and unstable until it cannot stand anymore, and what's left of the once-strong structure comes crashing down.

You're crashing down now, or you're pretty close to it. You're feeling the conflict, the restlessness, the stress of it all, and the rising tension in your life. And since you started reading this book, you might have already started seeing the different programs that are running your life.

But are you ready to leap? Are you ready to live intentionally? Are you ready to rediscover and realign with your authentic purpose?

Before you move into the first quadrant, let's dig into those feelings.

- Are there specific parts of your life that feel misaligned?

- Where do you feel like you're trying to just "make it work"?

- How does that affect you? How does that run over into other aspects of your life?

What if you changed that? What if instead of going along with the program you rewrote it?

Chapter 5

CONVEYOR BELT: MOVING BUT GOING NOWHERE

Two fish are swimming up a creek. The water is high and flowing, so it's hard, but the fish are fighting the current and doing their best. They're making small gains. But also, they can't stop. If they do, they'll get swept away. And they're not alone. All the other fish they see are also working hard to swim upstream.

A third fish swims up to the first two and says, "Hey, guys, this is actually the wrong way. It's so much easier if you turn around and go downstream."

"No, you're crazy," the first fish says.

"Yeah, if you turn around, the rocks come at you faster. You could get knocked off course so easily," the second fish says.

"This way we can see the twigs and rocks. We know what's coming," the first fish adds.

"Plus, we've been swimming upstream our entire lives," the second fish says. "I don't think I'd even know how to swim the other way."

"Suit yourselves," the third fish says. He turns around and begins flying down the creek.

Most of us work very hard to conform. We see what everyone around us is doing, and no matter what we think about it, we usually go along with it. We swim against the current of our individual nature because everyone else is fighting their natural instincts, too, and we don't want to be the odd fish out. But it would be so much easier to just turn around and swim with the flow.

What keeps us working so hard against our nature?

It's fear—installed in us through programming.

Some of this fear is instinctual and meant to keep us alive—think fight-or-flight response. Some of it is cultural—think spending money on college and getting an office job sitting eight hours a day at a computer. And while some of this programming serves us well (being alive and having a job), much of it does not because it tells us to live against our nature. It doesn't take our unique purpose into account.

For example, we're told to listen to our gut, but if our gut tells us to become an actor instead of an accountant, someone is quick to point out that it's a terrible idea. *You won't make any money. You won't have health insurance. Your life will be unstable.* So while the advice may come from a place of love, we're also being taught to *not* trust our gut.

Why do people tell us things like that? Sometimes it comes from their own programming; sometimes it's to keep us safe. *Survive over thrive.* The problem with this kind of programming is that other people can't possibly know what our unique purpose is. When we were born, we didn't come with a manual created specifically about us and how to nurture the parts of our personality that would help us manifest our purpose in this world. You are the only person who can know and understand your purpose.

However, you may be so stuck in your own programming and conditioning that you don't know what your purpose is. Or maybe you do know or at least have an idea of your purpose, but the gap between here and there feels like an impossibly wide chasm to cross.

As someone who's crossed it, I can tell you it's not impossible. You just need to build the bridge. And how do you build that bridge? You learn to recognize your programming and untangle your purpose from it.

CONFORMITY IS A DIS-EASE

When I started working with NLP, I felt like my life was finally being explained in a way that made sense. I also felt empowered to change, to bring my life and purpose into alignment, and to live the life of conviction I'd felt in my heart—felt but had been working very hard to ignore. I could finally see the Conveyor Belt I was on and understand how to get off of it.

I call the first quadrant in the Path of Purpose the Conveyor Belt Quadrant because once you're born, it carries you through life more quickly than you want it to. It doesn't stop moving, and it feels impossible to get off. If you do manage to exit the belt, you fall down from the nonmoving ground's lack of momentum. If you are going to find and follow your purpose, you must get off the Conveyor Belt. You must recognize your conditioning and stop conforming.

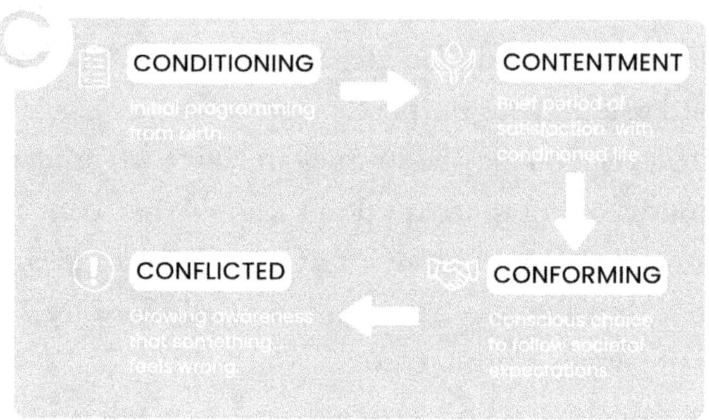

To some extent, **Conditioning** is easy to pinpoint. Think about it. You're being conditioned all the time in subtle ways through communication and language—what is said and how it's said. Advertisements persuade you to buy certain things and do certain things. Your religious and political associations tell you to believe certain principles and live in certain ways. If you reflect on your childhood, you'll see how your parents raised you with specific beliefs and thoughts about the world. That is all conditioning.

I want to reiterate something I mentioned in Chapter 2. Conditioning in and of itself is not bad. It's merely the installation of the programs—the thoughts and behavior patterns—that run our lives, the programming of the unconscious mind. Your unconscious mind is like a computer; it only runs on programs and scripts. It's not concerned with thinking. Most of the time, we don't get to choose the programming that runs our lives because it was installed when we were babies and children too young to understand what was happening.

And again, in pointing out the ways your life has been constructed and influenced, I'm not telling you to tear it all down. I'm merely pointing out what it is so you can start to see how and why you made the decisions that have led to where you are today. I'm going to make some assumptions here and say that for the most part, your conditioning has served you well. You may not be happy or satisfied at this moment, but you made it through school or earned your GED, most likely have a job and a place to live, and have food on the table. If you were looking at Maslow's hierarchy of needs, you'd see your physiological and safety needs are met.

Within that time, you were also content. Otherwise you would have started your search for answers earlier. Again, it's okay that you were content. I'm glad you were content. I was content, too, for a while. Most of us were. **Contentment** is that period when you don't have a lot of fear and worry. So your conditioning still worked. Maybe it even helped you get started as an adult. You chose a career and a place to live, it gave you some direction, and all felt good. But then you left the feel-good times of contentment and moved into **Conforming**.

The difference between conforming and being content with our conditioning is that conforming is a conscious act. It's looking around and seeing what others are doing and choosing to live the same way as everyone else around you even if you don't like it. It often looks like this: You drive to work and then grumble about the junk you have to do (your job). Then you commiserate with your colleagues at the coffee pot in the kitchenette. *Can you believe what your manager is having so-and-so do? So inefficient and a waste of time.* After a long day sitting in front of a computer trying not to fall asleep, you go home, have dinner, and do it all over again the next day, just like everyone else.

It's like the opening scenes of the 1990 movie *Joe Versus the Volcano*. Tom Hanks drives to work in a line of cars, trudges into an industrial building in a line of people all dressed like him in boring brown suits and coats, sits in a concrete room with bad fluorescent lighting, and stares at a lamp with a Hawaiian shade, daydreaming about taking a trip or changing his life.

Sure, you may also talk or think about doing something different, but you've never seen anyone leave their job and go do the thing they *actually* want to do. You may have had that one weird aunt or uncle who quit their job and became a yoga or surf instructor in Costa Rica, but that's not a real thing people do. It's a quirky family story.

But something has happened to shake you up or make you question your conformity. Maybe you had a health scare like Joe, or maybe you spoke to your quirky aunt or uncle over a Zoom chat or woke up one day and asked yourself how you became so bored and miserable with life. Now you are **Conflicted** because something (or everything) feels wrong. You may not know why you're conflicted. You just are.

This inner conflict is an emotion-heavy place to be. You feel at dis-ease. You may feel an absence of control. There's not a lot of discovery in this subquadrant, just more questions than answers. You've done everything you were supposed to do, and yet you're not fulfilled and happy. You're in a frustratingly vague endurance test. Do you persist in everything you've been doing, or do you explore these conflicted emotions more intentionally?

If you decide to persist, everything will stay the same.

If you explore, you'll most likely experience additional difficult emotions, but in my experience, that discomfort will fuel your search for something better. It's the Tony Robbins quote playing out in real time in your life: *"Change happens when the pain of staying the same is greater than the pain of change."*

Remember, you're on your way to living the best version of your life. Isn't that worth the pain?

CONDITIONING: WHERE IT ALL BEGINS

Conditioning, the initial programming of the human mind, begins at birth and extends through the early formative years. That is when your understanding of the world, yourself, and your place in life are entirely shaped by external forces—family dynamics, cultural norms, educational systems, and environmental factors. Your child-mind is absorbing and internalizing those early inputs without discrimination or conscious participation, creating the basic framework through which all your future experiences will be filtered and establishing your fundamental patterns of behavior and responses.

That also establishes the basic templates for your relationships, communication styles, and social expectations that will initially guide all your future interactions, shaping how you interact and interpret social situations. It is a one-time installation of basic programming that, once complete, can never be fully erased or experienced again. Further, these programs create the baseline from which all your future growth or limitation will proceed.

Through this unconscious absorption of worldviews, behaviors, and beliefs, your life and understanding are set. You adopt your family's religious practices, mirror your parents' emotional responses, and internalize your community's values without questioning or analyzing. You develop neural pathways and form the unconscious foundation of personality and perspective. While your eventual growth may add to, modify, or challenge these conditioned patterns, it can never completely erase them. Even now, I find some of this unconscious programming surfacing in unexpected ways, especially if I'm stressed or going through a challenge. However, I can now see it for what it is and move on. And you will be able to as well. That is why personal transformation takes so much effort. You're not working with a blank slate; it's quite the opposite. You're working with existing programming.

For someone like the Dalai Lama, conditioning played an extreme role in his development and upbringing. Identified at age two as the Buddha's reincarnation, he was removed from his family and immersed in an intensive environment of Buddhist teaching and traditional training. These established patterns of thought and behavior influenced his entire life's path, demonstrating how comprehensive and permanent early conditioning can be. While he would later develop his own understanding and interpretation of his role, the fundamental patterns established during his conditioning phase remain an integral part of his development.

Conditioning cannot be prevented or erased. However, its influence can be recognized and understood. In fact, identifying and examining these conditioned patterns is crucial for personal growth.

CONTENTMENT: NOTHING GOLD CAN STAY

After the initial period of conditioning, you naturally move into Contentment, a distinct and fleeting period in human development that occurs before you face the conscious choice to conform. Think back to when you were happiest, perhaps it was late childhood to early adolescence, the time you had your last taste of genuine, *unexamined* satisfaction with life as it is. You probably had a natural ease of being, simply existing within your conditioned patterns without questioning them and finding simple joy and satisfaction in living according to the only way you knew how. Like conditioning, once you leave contentment, you can never return.

In young people, this form of contentment manifests as a natural comfort within their conditioned existence. You might remember times when you felt complete satisfaction in your life, your school routine, and your place in your friend group without feeling the pressure to question or alter anything about your life. This contentment is pure because it exists before the awakening of social consciousness and the recognition of alternative ways of being. Right now, interactions with others are genuine and authentic—engagement without self-consciousness, without social calculation, and without conscious poisoning.

Historical records show that Emily Dickinson was a bright, socially engaged child who found genuine satisfaction in her early life and education before she withdrew from society. She experienced a period of simple contentment within her family's structured but comfortable world. That natural contentment contrasted sharply with her conscious choice to withdraw from society, marking the clear distinction between the innocent satisfaction of youth and the more complex choices of adult life. Once lost to the demands of conscious social navigation, contentment cannot be truly regained in its original form.

While this stage cannot be maintained indefinitely, its memory serves an important purpose in personal development. It becomes a touchstone we return to when we begin searching for our lost authenticity later in life. As we grow, this last moment of pure living becomes overshadowed by the conscious navigation of social expectations.

CONFORMING: DUCK, DUCK, ~~GOOSE~~ DUCK

Conforming represents the first conscious choice in human development—a decision to align with established social patterns and expectations. Unlike the unconscious absorption of conditioning or the innocent contentment of youth, conforming emerges as a strategic response to the realization that society rewards certain behaviors and punishes others. Many people adopt the behaviors and thought patterns developed in this stage for the rest of their lives. In fact, you were there for a while, maybe a long while, before paying attention to the dissatisfaction you felt. Had you chosen to ignore your discontent, bottle it up, and place it on a dusty shelf in your heart, it would have become your permanent life position. After all, conforming offers the compelling combination of social acceptance, predictable outcomes, and a clear road map for navigating life's complexities—whether or not you like it.

What does it look like? Turn to your left and then turn to your right. You'll see people adopting socially sanctioned paths and behaviors such as pursuing a traditional career followed by conventional relationship patterns, and maintaining accepted social practices. People do that because those patterns provide reliable results, not because they've deeply examined those choices. You can often achieve significant success within these established frameworks and avoid most, if not all, risks associated with questioning your choices. You can also develop strong social bonds, often forged through the mutual commiseration caused by conformity. But these relationships may eventually become the bonds holding you back from journeying the Path of Purpose, despite the comfort they provide.

If you recall, I did this for decades, and it always felt like trying to jam a square peg into a round hole. I had to shave down my edges to fit through that hole more times than I care to remember, but the discomfort of changing my shape eventually led me here.

If you choose to conform for the rest of your life, to continue chiseling yourself into the right shape, well, this way of life limits your potential for deeper fulfillment or broader impact. While you'll eventually master and maintain societal norms, just know you're trading security for deeper authenticity.

While some will naturally progress beyond this stage through disillusionment or inner calling, they will return to it repeatedly as a safe harbor after venturing into questioning or personal exploration. However, I want to be clear. This is not a failure of development but a conscious choice that prioritizes stability and social integration over personal expansion or authentic self-expression. And that can be okay. But you're reading this book because it's not okay for you any longer. You're tired of returning to this place. You're looking for a road map to escape the gravitational pull of conformity.

Let's look at Warren Buffett. Despite his extraordinary success, he has maintained notably conformist patterns in his personal life. Living in the same modest house since 1958, maintaining simple eating habits (including a well-documented preference for everyday American foods), and advocating for conventional investment strategies, Buffett exemplifies how someone can achieve remarkable success while embracing conformity in many areas of life. And he loves it. It's a fine life for him. But despite occasional ventures into other quadrants (Enlightenment, Impact) through his business innovations, Buffett consistently returns to and appears most comfortable with conventional patterns in his personal life.

Conforming represents a legitimate life strategy that for many provides sufficient satisfaction and security to sustain them throughout their lives. While it may limit the achievement of full potential or the experience of deeper purpose, it offers a perfectly acceptable path through life that millions find adequate for their needs and comfortable for their temperament. (If you want to try to become the next Warren Buffet, by all means please do. But if you really were going to do that, you probably would have already done it. So keep reading.)

CONFLICTED: WELCOME TO THE SHOW

If you've come this far, you are most likely in the last subquadrant of the Conveyor Belt: Conflicted, or the first subquadrant of Deconstruction: Disenchantment. Either way, you're mired in the state of tension that arises when the comfort of conformity chafes against your growing awareness of conformity's limitations. This internal friction between your conforming behaviors and your awakening sense that something more might be possible arrives uninvited, creating a persistent discomfort that demands either resolution or suppression. You are facing a crucial turning point between maintaining comfortable patterns and acknowledging growing doubts. You are standing on the precipice before taking the leap into active questioning where internal tension builds to a point that you can no longer ignore it.

This Conflict feels like a growing sense of restlessness or unease in your life. You're maintaining your conventional job, relationships, and social positions while experiencing increasing anxiety about your authenticity. Unlike Conformity, there is no stable but limited satisfaction here. If you stay too long in Conflict, the psychological strain can manifest as increasing anxiety, depression, or physical symptoms that affect all areas of your life.

The energy required to maintain external conformity while wrestling with internal doubts eventually takes its toll. You will be forced to move toward questioning, or you will have to create increasingly sophisticated forms of self-deception. Personally, I started experiencing increased insomnia, lying awake at night questioning my choices, and feeling trapped between the security of my life and an undefined but persistent sense that I was meant for something different. My external compliance constantly clashed with my growing internal doubt.

This internal conflict inevitably affects relationships and social interactions. You might find yourself withdrawing from previously comfortable social situations, feeling an increasing sense of isolation. Your interactions may become tinged with a subtle inauthenticity as the gap widens between your external presentation and your internal experience.

To move forward, you must eventually face the source of your conflict. You must either recommit to conformity with a full awareness of its limitations (choose to stay on the Conveyor Belt) or take the first steps toward questioning your conditioned patterns (enter Deconstruction).

A good example of this is author John Steinbeck. During his early adult years, he worked as a caretaker and tour guide at Lake Tahoe, trying to conform to conventional expectations. His letters from this period reveal deep internal conflict between maintaining a "respectable" job and his burning desire to write. The conflict manifested as physical illness and depression until he finally embraced his calling as a writer.

Conflict is the crucial gateway between conscious acceptance of Conformity and conscious questioning of Deconstruction. No matter where you go from here, you will have a certain level of discomfort. If you turn back to Conformity, you can work hard to forget the calling for authentic living in your heart. And sometimes that works. If you move forward, your pain will grow worse for a while as you break apart the scaffolding that's holding up your current life. But at some point, you'll come out the other side feeling more alive than you ever imagined possible and helping other people live better lives too.

WHAT MAKES YOU TICK?

Conditioning and conforming taught me that I needed to go to college, get married young, and then find a good job to support my family. For a business- and numbers-minded kid like me, I ended up staying on with the corporate finance team where I interned. Obviously, I was the youngest and newest person in the office, and the next most junior-level employee had been with the company for over ten years. Even at that early stage, that didn't sit well with me.

I thought to myself, *If I stay here, I can expect to do the same thing forever.*

I felt bad about that. I felt hollow. That wasn't exciting to me at all. I knew I didn't want to stare at spreadsheets and financial profit and loss statements for the different cost centers in the company for the next forty years. So I became conflicted.

Yet I didn't know what else to do. I was good at that job. I was getting paid well. I thought at least part of the world kind of needed that work. And everyone was proud of me for landing such a great opportunity so early in my career. They all felt like my life was set. But I didn't.

Not knowing what else to do, though, I was embedded in the idea of a traditional career track for many years. I planned to perform my role well for a while, rack up a few good annual reviews, and then apply for and win a promotion to middle management. I'd work in middle management for a while (probably twice as long as my junior role), do a good job, hopefully get promoted, and so on.

My life was a pendulum swinging between Contentment and Conflict until . . . well, you know the rest. Like so many people, I conformed to my conditioning for as long as I could until the pain of staying disconnected from my purpose grew so great that I had to change or I didn't know what would happen. You don't need to hit such a dramatic rock bottom to say it's time to figure this out, to say to yourself, "It's time to find the thing that makes me tick, makes my life bigger than just the four walls around me, and gives meaning to every moment I'm here."

At that point, you're either nodding along or throwing this book across the room—convinced and onboard or frustrated and defensive. When I learned about mental programming, I was relieved because it meant I could change my life, that I wouldn't be miserable forever, and that I wasn't *supposed* to be miserable forever. I also felt determined that I wouldn't let myself be miserable forever.

Seeking purpose isn't easy, though, and I knew I had a lot of unlearning to do to uncover my path. I would also need a lot of courage to follow it.

Checkpoint

Now knowing that there are programs driving everything you do, I want to pose some questions for your consideration. You don't need to be able to answer them right away. I'm not asking you to stop reading and agonize over the *whys* driving your life. I just want you to read these questions and ponder them as they come up for you.

- Are you living a life you love—one that feels totally aligned inside and out?
  - If not, why?

- Were you on course to be aligned and then changed your mind?
  - Why?

- Is something holding you back from changing your life?
  - What?

In asking these questions, we're starting the process of pinpointing the programming that has driven your actions to this point. We're also beginning the work of uncovering your purpose, something we'll dive into at a deeper level through Discovery in Chapter 6.

As you find the answers to these questions, hold yourself back from making any judgments about them and how they make you angry, sad, confused, frustrated, or something else.

Right now, we're mostly concerned with understanding why we do what we do and why we did what we did—not about the outcome. When we know the why, we can tap into a conscious decision-making process and then start to shift our behaviors to align our lives with our purpose rather than act out of unconscious programming.

Chapter 6

DECONSTRUCTION: UNCOVERING WHAT MAKES YOU TICK

In 1832, Ralph Waldo Emerson went through a crisis of faith and resigned from his role as pastor of a Unitarian church. As with all crises, no single catalyst triggered Emerson's questioning of his faith; rather, a series of "whys" accumulated, ultimately leading to his departure from the church—disagreements about communion, public prayer, and essentially the conscious choice to not do things the way they'd always been done just because. Less than ten years later, he wrote the essay "Self-Reliance" where he stated, "A foolish consistency is the hobgoblin of little minds, adored by little statesmen and philosophers and divines."[3] He questioned the idea of conforming for the sake of conforming. To him, it was the Conveyor Belt of organized religion, not an authentic expression of faith. So he left.

I'm not saying that people must abandon their faith to discover their purpose. This story simply illustrates how asking "why" can lead a person from Conflict to Discontentment, then to Despair, and finally to a Determination to find what is missing.

These feelings often lead to dramatic action such as leaving your profession or faith. In fact, in his spirit of interrogation, Emerson said this to the Harvard Divinity School graduating class of 1836: "Let me admonish you, first of all, to go alone; to refuse the good models, even those most sacred in the imagination of men, and dare to love God without mediator or veil."[4]

Go it alone. Refuse the models. Love God the way you need to love God. While Emerson was talking about finding your own way in faith, it's equally applicable to the idea of letting go of what and who the world tells you to be and finding the purpose that was planted in your heart. Dig down to explore the disconnect in your life. In other words, jump off the Conveyor Belt and embrace your own path.

Once you've moved through the Conveyor Belt Quadrant, there is absolutely no way to ignore the conformity in your life or the programming running your life. The more you try to push the feelings of conflict away, the more you'll see how the life you're leading isn't the one meant for you; it's the product of everything outside of you forcing you into a specific path that's acceptable to others. That doesn't make it a bad life, just not the life you were created to live. This was all covered in Chapter 5, so we don't need to revisit it ad nauseam. It's enough that you recognize the feeling. But you still have a choice: You can accept this hand-me-down life and be miserable knowing that there is a better one out there, one that is meant for only you, or you can dive into deconstructing the systems in your life to reconstruct it around your ikigai.

If you want to go with the first choice, go ahead and close this book. Give it to your friend or neighbor. Maybe they're ready for their purpose and something better. Or leave it on the lunch table at your office where another miserable person searching for life might find it and use it to become the most fulfilled version of themselves.

Or instead, take a deep breath and settle in as I guide you through the toughest yet most invigorating of the quadrants—toughest because Deconstruction asks a lot from you emotionally, requiring resilience and perseverance to come out the other side. It's invigorating because once you hit Determination and Discovering, you will feel more alive than maybe you ever have been.

DECONSTRUCTION IN REAL LIFE

You know you've entered the Deconstruction Quadrant when you begin consciously questioning and examining the inherited and installed patterns and beliefs in your life. This quadrant represents the crucial phase where you'll begin to recognize and challenge your conditioning. You're here to methodically examine, question, and dismantle previously accepted truths. That is the work of Deconstruction.

Throughout this quadrant, you move through stages of increasing awareness and active questioning, progressing from initial Discontentment through Despair until you become determined to seek and discover new possibilities. This progression represents the necessary breakdown of inherited frameworks, creating space for authentic growth and development. Deconstruction is the bridge between unconscious acceptance and conscious creation.

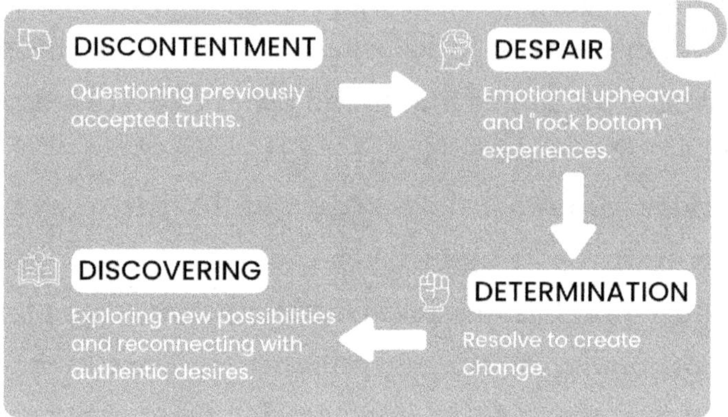

That being said, it's impossible to predict how much time you will need to move through Discontentment and Despair. Why is this important to mention? Because your will to keep moving forward will wax and wane, and your belief that this is all worth it will be tested. But the work you do here becomes the foundation for all future authentic development as it clears away limiting beliefs and patterns that would otherwise restrict growth. So when it gets tough, when you want to quit, just remember that you're making space for something better, for the life that's meant to be yours. In all honesty, I hated this quadrant, or at least I hated the subquadrants of **Discontentment** and **Despair**, but I'm grateful for all of it. Without the pain, I would never have moved forward into the life I have now.

I entered Discontentment and began questioning my beliefs and life choices around my first pivot in 2012, but I stayed stuck between the Conveyor Belt and Deconstruction for a few more years. Around 2015 or 2016, two years before we left on the RV trip and when I started dissecting my political philosophy, I finally fully embraced Deconstruction. I asked every question I could to drive down to the root of my Discontentment, which eventually led to the desperation of the RV trip I wrote about at the beginning of the book.

Even still, while I thought uprooting my life would help me answer or at least satisfy the never-ending questions, it led instead to more questions and eventually my descent into Despair. Despair is a pit, a swamp, quicksand. It's *The Lord of the Rings: The Two Towers*—Frodo and Sam traveling through the stinking Dead Marshes full of fallen warriors, and Frodo falling into the water and being pulled down into the darkness by the ghosts. But instead of Sam pulling me out, I had to figure out how to save myself.

Once I asked all the questions and came up with empty answers, I didn't know what to do. I was at a new level of low. I couldn't see the light at the end of the tunnel because there wasn't one—just more darkness. That was about the time we ended the RV trip and returned home. Abby and I had to decide how we were going to move forward, which involved my moving out for a few months.

You can become mired in Despair, but you can also become *inspired* by Despair. I know it sounds impossible and like something people say because it rhymes and sounds good, but it's true. When you have hit Despair, you are as low as you can go. And once you're at the bottom, it's the cliché: The only way to go is up.

Packing my clothes and shampoo into bags, my laptop and notebooks for work into boxes, and not knowing when I would be back under the same roof with Abby and the kids was as low as I could ever go. It was the unimaginable come to pass.

But as I backed my car out of the driveway, I became **Determined**. I knew I would find the solution because that wasn't how my life was going to go. I knew I loved Abby. We knew we wanted to be a family together, not a family apart. We just didn't know what it would take to get there. So like any adventuring hero, I set off on the journey to **Discovering** the path that would lead me back home.

DISCONTENTMENT: CLARITY OF DISSATISFACTION

Discontentment marks the initial awakening from the spell of conformity. It represents the first stage of conscious questioning of previously accepted patterns and beliefs. You are moving from passive acceptance to active examination of your life's fundamental assumptions. Unlike the internal conflict that preceded it, Discontentment brings a clear, often painful recognition that the established systems and beliefs you have trusted may not be entirely valid or valuable. This stage arrives like dawn breaking after a long night, illuminating familiar landscapes in ways that make them suddenly appear strange and less reliable than they once seemed.

In practice, Discontentment manifests as a profound shift in your perspective regarding previously accepted truths. You might suddenly see the arbitrary nature of social conventions you once took for granted, recognize the limitations of your chosen career path, or question the religious or cultural beliefs you've held since childhood. This awakening feels both liberating and disturbing as the comfort of certainty gives way to the challenge of questioning.

At this point on the journey, I felt guilty, shameful, disrespectful, and scared—terrified, even. I felt guilty because my family had always been there for me, and now I was interrogating their intentions. I was shameful because I felt like the mere act of asking questions seemed like a rejection of my life. I felt disrespectful because of all the above. I was scared and terrified because, well, I just didn't know where all this would lead.

You are entering a destabilizing period of life. As the frameworks you've always trusted begin to show cracks, you will probably experience a period of profound uncertainty similar to what I just described. That stage can affect everything from career choices to personal relationships to how you interact with people still fully invested in conventional systems. While that can be uncomfortable, it is the controlled brush fire clearing the way for new saplings of inspiration and authenticity.

During this blaze, you may feel like you're on an emotional roller-coaster. You may feel an increasing fear of losing foundational beliefs. Relationships may become strained as you, the discontented person, can no longer fully participate in the shared illusions or comfortable assumptions of your outdated programming. You may begin to feel isolated as you see through social conventions while still needing to navigate them for practical purposes. You may resist your growing knowledge and hold on as tightly as possible to the illusions in your life. But at some point, they will turn into smoke and slip through your grasping hands.

I remember this all too well. While I was questioning my religion and relationship with God, I was still actively going to church every Sunday and participating in my church community throughout the week. At times I felt like a fraud. But eventually, all those questions led to a deeper understanding of my relationship with God and my church, and a deeper, stronger faith.

To move through this stage effectively, you need to learn to balance your growing awareness with practical necessity. It's not about wholesale rejection of all your previous beliefs and systems but about developing the capacity to examine them critically while maintaining functional engagement with the world. That requires developing a kind of double vision—seeing both the constructed nature of social systems and their practical utility.

While Emerson's crisis of faith and growing discontent led to his resignation from the Unitarian church, it ultimately led to his emergence as a pioneering voice in American Transcendentalism. He had to dismantle the beliefs passed down to him from his father, his father's father, and so on in order to find his own worldview. His experience exemplifies how discontentment can serve as a gateway to more authentic forms of expression and understanding.

Discontentment represents a crucial step toward authentic living, though it initially feels more like losing ground than gaining it. Like removing old wallpaper, this process reveals what lies beneath surface appearances, creating the possibility for genuine choice rather than mere acceptance. But before you can reach that deeper layer, that authentic expression of who you are, you have to travel through those Dead Marshes of Despair.

DESPAIR: THE ROCK BOTTOM BEFORE THE CLIMB

Despair follows Discontentment as a more active and emotionally charged stage of Deconstruction. Unlike the intellectual awakening of Discontentment, Despair manifests as a visceral dissatisfaction with the status quo, so much so that the emotion becomes a powerful driver for change. Where Discontentment opens your eyes, Despair stirs your heart, creating an increasingly unbearable tension between what is and what could be, making it difficult to maintain old patterns.

As you move through this emotional state, you will begin to actively dismantle the comfortable structures of Conforming because your growing restlessness cannot be easily suppressed or ignored. The farther you move into Despair, the more dissatisfaction you will feel with previously acceptable circumstances. For example, your once-satisfying job will become increasingly intolerable, your social circles will feel increasingly shallow, and your daily routines will become increasingly meaningless. Your ability to maintain comfortable social facades will begin to break down. Small talk becomes painful, social obligations feel burdensome, and the disparity between internal reality and external expectations becomes increasingly difficult to bridge. That often leads to a period of social withdrawal or seeking out others who are experiencing similar dissatisfaction. You may be forced to either retreat to conformity or push forward to more active changes.

Emotionally, you may be feeling overwhelmed. You may have increased anxiety about the changes you know you'll need to make, even if you don't know exactly what those changes are. You may also be resisting your feelings of deep dissatisfaction with life. But the emotional energy from Discontentment to Despair often provides the necessary fuel for significant life changes.

I found myself pulling back from my social circles out of shame about not knowing who I was. I didn't know how to be around the people I typically had normal relationships with. I also began noticing that every time we interact with someone, we don't typically show our truest selves. We behave in the way we think *they* think we should behave. This was a classic case of perception being projection rather than reality. For me, since every major pillar of my life's foundation was cracked and felt like it was crumbling, I didn't know how to be. That also confused the way I thought they thought I should be. I didn't want to come off as a fraud or a fake. But I also didn't have the energy at that point to fabricate and prolong the wearing of a mask. So it was easier to just not engage at all.

Along with the emotional upheaval, you could begin to experience physical symptoms such as sleepless nights, unexplained anxiety, or a constant sense of restlessness as the growing gap between external circumstances and internal desires creates a persistent discomfort that demands attention. In other words, you will most likely enter a bit of a depression. That is why I described it as the Dead Marshes. For a while, you may try to navigate around these deep wells of hopelessness as Frodo tried to stick to the path as Gollum advised. But if you turn your head ever so slightly, gaze into the water, and see your reflection wavering before you in the murky depths, you will fall in. And as terrible as that sounds, it's as it should be. You need to confront those systems and go through this emotionally charged and devastating state in order to move forward.

My Dead Marshes were riddled with hopelessness and fear. Everything in my life felt shaky; I had no firm foundation because nothing was firm. I couldn't even rely on my faith at that time since I was questioning the existence of God. But like Frodo and Sam, I had to keep moving forward if I was ever going to make it out.

In a sense, you're in the grieving stages of change—you may be feeling very real feelings of losing the life you once had or at least losing your feelings of security or stability. You may be shocked at seeing that things aren't what they seem to be. You might be in denial about your dissatisfaction with the life you're leading. You may be angry at yourself for going down this path or maybe at others for the influence they had over you. There might be bargaining—*can you still possibly make this work at all without having to change anything?* There could be depression because you know in your heart that the answer is no and it's too late to try to make things work as they are. You might experience testing—what might work now? Or maybe there's acceptance—in other words, you've decided to jump in with both feet for whatever might be next.

Remember the description of transforming into a *Super Saiyan* form in *Dragon Ball Z*? Right now you have collapsed in on yourself and are pulling in all the energy from the air around you as you undergo an internal metamorphosis. If you're going to get out of despair, you need to learn to harness your pain and hopelessness as motivation while not allowing it to become destructive. Transform that raw dissatisfaction into focused energy for change. How? Develop the ability to sit with uncomfortable emotions while beginning to explore potential alternatives to current circumstances. Do something to break your patterns enough to see them for what they are and where they originate. Many people achieve that through meditation practices, yoga, lifting weights, or activities where you have to push yourself physically and in the process end up breaking through mental barriers and doing things you'd never thought possible before.

When she was a young, single mother, Maya Angelou worked many dead-end jobs to support her son. Her growing Discontentment and Despair with the limitations of her circumstances, particularly during her time as a nightclub dancer and restaurant cook, created the emotional pressure that eventually drove her toward her true calling as a writer and performer. That period of intense dissatisfaction, while challenging, provided the emotional fuel necessary for her eventual transformation into one of America's most significant literary voices. Her experience shows how Despair, though painful, can serve as a crucial motivator for authentic self-expression and meaningful change.

Despair, while uncomfortable, serves as a necessary force to break free from stagnant patterns. Like water pressure building behind a dam, the buildup of emotional energy leads to significant life changes.

DETERMINATION: THE ONLY WAY OUT IS THROUGH

Determination emerges as the first constructive stage in the Deconstruction Quadrant. It marks a crucial shift from emotional rejection to purposeful action and moves from the burning dissatisfaction of *what is* to a powerful commitment to *what could be*. Where Discontentment creates the emotional pressure for change, Determination provides the disciplined force to make that change possible. As the bridge between the rejection of old patterns and the discovery of new possibilities, Determination is the first stage where you begin to harness your emotional energy productively rather than simply experiencing it as distress.

What does this look like? It's a steely resolve to create change regardless of immediate circumstances or obvious solutions. It's the emergence of clear intention, even though the path forward isn't fully visible. You might begin taking concrete steps toward change such as enrolling in evening classes, saving money for a career transition, or systematically developing new skills without yet having a complete picture of your final destination. No matter what, you'll feel a shift in energy from restless anxiety to focused action, even if that action initially seems small in scope.

However, while you might be feeling more hopeful, stronger, or just less depressed, there will still be tough emotions and obstacles that pop up. You might fear commitment to any specific direction; after all, you committed your life to the wrong direction, so how do you know this new one will be any different? You might fear failure or fear failing to change. You might have anxiety about the practical implications of change, which could lead you back to familiar emotional patterns that in turn impede your ability to change. You could get stuck in a victim or critic mentality. You're at a crossroads here, and making no choice is still a choice.

On my own journey, the Determination phase was a galvanizing time of action. After my first pivot around 2012 when I left the traditional corporate world to start my own business, I was energized by the idea of finally finding my path in life. That sense of endless possibility I had as a kid returned. I was optimistic about everything. Even though it was a tough transition—starting a business takes a lot of work—it was worth it.

The second time I entered Determination somewhere around 2022, action felt more urgent, and I had a stronger resolve to find the right (or next right) path for my life because there was more at stake. Abby and I were on shaky ground. My business had failed. Everything was falling apart. I was falling apart—or so it felt. But even in light of everything, I was filled with a sense of purpose that made those circumstances more bearable because I knew they weren't permanent.

And that Determination will change your life. It will significantly alter how you interact with your environment and relationships. Instead of withdrawing, which you may have done in Despair, you will begin to strategically engage with your situation, seeing it as a temporary platform from which to launch change rather than a permanent prison to escape from. That can lead to improved relationships as your desperate energy of Discontentment is replaced by purposeful engagement.

To move forward into the Discovery phase, you must learn to balance your newfound resolve with practical wisdom and patience—maintain determination while developing the discernment to direct it effectively. That requires learning to sustain focused effort over time while remaining flexible enough to adjust strategies as new information and opportunities emerge.

In 1985, the board of Apple forced Steve Jobs out of his role with the company. But rather than succumb to bitterness or defeat, Jobs channeled his energy into new ventures, founding NeXT Computer, acquiring Pixar, and learning and honing the skills he needed to be a great leader and effective innovator. His determination during that period wasn't just about proving others wrong; it was about pursuing his vision and growing personally and professionally despite significant setbacks. Jobs's experience shows how Determination can provide the sustained energy needed to bridge the gap between rejecting current circumstances and discovering new horizons.

You're at a crucial transition from reactive to proactive engagement with life's challenges. Use this time to grow and learn and figure out what you need to do to get to the next step—creating a plan. Like a river finding its course after a flood, you are beginning to channel the powerful emotions of earlier stages into productive directions. Determination can transform setbacks into opportunities for innovation and growth through the power of focused resolve in creating new possibilities from apparent defeat. You are now ready for meaningful change.

DISCOVERING: REAWAKENING TO LIFE AND ALL ITS POSSIBILITIES

Discovering represents the final stage of Deconstruction, marking the transition from determined action to expansive exploration. This phase opens you up to a state of active curiosity and experimental engagement with new possibilities. It transforms your linear drive of determination into a more organic process of exploration and insight. Where Determination provides the force to break free from old patterns, Discovering creates the space to envision and explore new ones. There's also an air of acceptance that things are now different because you can see the programming. It's the end of a mourning period where you start to accept the new normal, and the keenness of the pain gives way to an allowance of new thought.

At this point, you may be remembering dreams you had as a kid or teenager, reengaging with long-forgotten but life-giving hobbies and renewing and nurturing parts of yourself or your personality that you'd consciously rejected because they didn't fit the Conveyor Belt version of your life. You will probably smile more, have ideas again, and feel new in some respects. Embrace it as a time of celebration and joy as you begin the process of building the life you actually want, the one that was always meant for you.

As the bridge between the dismantling work of Deconstruction and the constructive potential of the Enlightenment Quadrant, Discovering is both a culmination and a gateway. The energy you once spent fighting old patterns can now be directed toward exploring new horizons, and your focused intention from Determination expands into broader exploration.

Don't be surprised if you feel a curiosity about life's possibilities beyond conventional boundaries. You may find yourself daydreaming and actually planning how to become a surf instructor in Costa Rica. You might join a running club. You may even sign up for acting and improv classes. The possibilities are endless because you are limitless. Welcome back your childlike sense of wonder, and embrace it from your mature point of view and purpose.

For me, I went through Determination and Discovering twice—that first pivot in 2012 when I started my first business and again after the RV experience where everything fell apart. The first pivot revealed to me that I liked and was good at building businesses. The second in 2022 showed me I wanted to find a way to help others (more on that in Chapter 8). Only by putting these parts together could I create a life built on my authentic purpose and lean into ikigai. But it all started with giving myself the chance to discover my innate gifts and desires.

While everything may feel exciting and new again, you may still experience periods of fear—fear of losing momentum as you explore, fear about wasting time and resources, or fear of making wrong decisions. Exploring can also invoke anxiety about not having a clear direction. You may have flashbacks to high school or college when you didn't have an answer to these questions: "What do you want to be when you grow up?" and "How are you going to make a living doing X, Y, Z?" It seems impractical. You may also get hung up on old programming about what you're supposed to have or get out of life, things like a job that provides a 401(k) and health insurance or being tied down with a mortgage or car payment. That is the time to stand firm in your resolve to follow your intuition.

When you need inspiration, remember Julia Child. Having broken free from the conventional expectations for a woman of her background and era, Julia is the poster child of the Discovering phase. After she and her husband, Paul, moved to France, she leaned into her curiosity and passionate exploration of French cuisine and culture. She learned the language and enrolled in classes at Le Cordon Bleu at a time when women didn't become chefs. Rather than being discouraged by the obstacles oftentimes intentionally put in her way, she persisted in her journey and purpose of bringing French food and cooking to America. Her initial displacement transformed into a profound personal and professional revelation that reshaped her life and the American culinary culture, illustrating how Discovering can open up entirely new life paths that were unimaginable in previous frameworks of understanding.

Take heart knowing that as you explore, you will begin developing discernment about which discoveries merit deeper investigation. Like an explorer mapping unknown territory, you will begin to sketch out the potential landscape of a more authentic life. Stay open to new possibilities and cultivate the wisdom to recognize the meaningful opportunities among them.

COURAGE IS THE KEY TO DISCOVERING YOUR BEST LIFE

Deconstruction is not for the faint of heart. It is scary to question everything in your life. It's terrifying to make changes. It can feel impossible to step out into the unknown, unsure if it is actually the perfect next step. Here's a secret to getting through—and there is no perfect next step. Life is not a test to ace. It's not a competition against your neighbor. Yes, you can make a pros and cons lists. You can make plans. But in order to successfully navigate Deconstruction, you must have courage. You must be brave enough to try something and admit that maybe that's not the thing, or yes, that is the next thing. Then decide how to get there and take the next step in that direction.

When Emerson realized he had to leave his post with the church in order to move in the direction of his purpose, I can't imagine how hard that was. After all, in doing so, he was effectively rejecting tenets that upheld the Unitarian church. But had he ignored the stirrings in his heart, the questions swirling around his head, we wouldn't have Transcendental thought. If Maya Angelou ignored her calling to write, we wouldn't have "I Know Why the Caged Bird Sings." If Steve Jobs had wallowed in despair after being fired from the company he helped found, where would he be? If Julia Child had accepted the social standards that women didn't go to culinary school at that time, where would American haute cuisine be?

When you enter Deconstruction, you don't know where you'll end up. There's no way to know what impact your life will have on the world until you've lived it. Staying on the Conveyor Belt is not living. But asking why, leaning into the discomfort of seeking answers and exploring the calling in your heart will lead to discovering your most authentic life.

# Checkpoint

At some point on your journey, you will fall into a pit. You will hit rock bottom, but you will climb out using the ladder you build yourself. How will you build the ladder? You will build it by digging deep and discovering what makes you get out of bed every morning, by remembering and reconnecting with your passion and joy, and by pushing past doubt and fear and continuing to move forward.

I want to be very clear though. This is tough work. You might decide that you need to enlist the help of a coach or therapist to work through everything coming up for you. Get the help you need to keep going. I worked with several types of therapists before finding NLP. Remember that whatever you're feeling right now is valid. Those feelings are important, especially if they're uncomfortable or painful. They are the keys to unlocking your authentic self.

Before you read the next chapter, take a few minutes to reflect on the following questions:

- With your old beliefs and patterns cleared away, what new values or ways of being are springing up for you? You may have decided that some of the programmed ideas do speak to your authentic self, and so you may hold onto them. But what else is emerging?

  - When you have time, list your values and why they're important to you.

🖋 What hobbies or interests have you reconnected with?

- ○ If you don't remember any, try some new things—activities that spark your curiosity and just seem like fun. You never know what a dance class or intramural soccer team might do for your life. Or your new business partner or opportunity might be one art easel away.

🖋 What changes can you make today that will move you even one step closer to living an authentic life?

Right now your job is to dig into what gives you life and what makes you excited. Don't worry about how you can turn your passion into your job. Don't worry if you're doing this Discovery thing "right." The Conveyor Belt is the predetermined one-size-fits-all life that doesn't actually fit anyone at all. But there is no one-size-fits-all right way of living. What you're after is the "your-way-of-living" life.

As you turn the page, hold onto your newly found or newly remembered optimism. Anything is possible, but you have to be brave enough to make your own way.

ENLIGHTENMENT: CREATING YOUR AUTHENTIC LIFE

The first time I acknowledged that something was wrong with the direction of my life was in 2012. Before then, I knew it wasn't quite what I imagined, but that was okay—until the philosophical questions about life became overwhelming and the despair I felt was too much to ignore. That's when I knew I needed to express myself to someone. And that someone was my lovely sister.

In Chapter 3, I described our conversation about my life's purpose. While I'd always worked in business, I hadn't really thought about starting my own business. Yet that was the urgent call I felt in my heart at that time. *Start a business, and they will come.* (*Field of Dreams*, anyone?)

I knew that continuing on with the status quo wasn't the answer. I knew that trying to work for someone else or doing something else would leave me feeling just as unsatisfied and unfulfilled. I had to strike out and build something—something that came from me and was an expression of what I believed to be important. More than that, I needed to prove to myself that I could do this.

You know about my pivots in the 2010s and finding my direction in the early 2020s. But that was by no means a one-and-done (or twice-and-done) process. Even though I felt the calling, I still had to discover, experiment, and clear away all the external programming in my life in order to find my authentic purpose—ikigai—which frankly took more time than I liked.

In terms of ikigai, my initial pivot connected my profession with vocation and a sprinkle of passion (it's always a work of passion in the beginning). I was using my knowledge and experience to solve a problem in the world instead of just pushing paper around and building someone else's business. I learned so much from that pivot, mainly that I could build a successful business, that I loved building businesses, and that unless I'm helping others, eventually the business becomes just another thing I do. I was missing the sustained passion and mission.

I've said this before, and I'll say it again: There's no set amount of time people spend in any one quadrant. I bounced between the Deconstruction and Enlightenment Quadrants for about twelve years before I moved on to the Impact Quadrant. It was an invaluable time of growth, reconnecting with my inner sense of self and continuously building and rebuilding my life around the divinely appointed purpose I'd always carried with me. Step by step, I began living from within rather than from without. Every decision became easier as I listened to the voice inside that was guiding me. Some relationships blossomed even more, while others withered as a natural part of the transformative process of living from Enlightenment. But the best part of all was seeing how my new sense of living inspired others in my life to start exploring their authentic selves and subtly change their own lives for the better.

My best advice? It doesn't matter how long you stay in a quadrant. If you are learning, growing, and listening to your authentic self, then you're getting closer to your ikigai. And you'll know it when you feel it.

MEETING YOUR AUTHENTIC SELF

You have jumped off the Conveyor Belt. You've survived Deconstruction. Welcome to the rest of your life! It's not that the Enlightenment Quadrant is all sunshine and roses. You'll experience both internal and external shifts in your life, but everything will just feel easier, even the hard parts.

This is called the Enlightenment Quadrant because you have discovered your authentic self after clearing away all the programming that was hiding it from the world. You're beginning to live from your true core values, the ones that have always been inside you but that maybe you ignored. You're beginning to listen to them to make your decisions, and you're gaining confidence in your ability to make those decisions. You're Kevin Costner plowing up half of your cornfield to build a baseball diamond, even though everyone around you might think that's insane.

In the Deconstruction Quadrant, you tore down and cleared out inherited patterns of behavior and thought processes and began to ask yourself, "What do I really want? What do I really think about this? *Who am I really?*" That discovery moved you from exploring who you might be to knowing who you are. And now you've committed to living from that natural center.

You're building the foundation of your future life right now. You are an active creator of your authentic experience rather than a passive questioner. Your authentic self can emerge through recognition, expression, and integration. Understanding and embracing this challenge is the prerequisite for the sustained freedom of the Impact Quadrant.

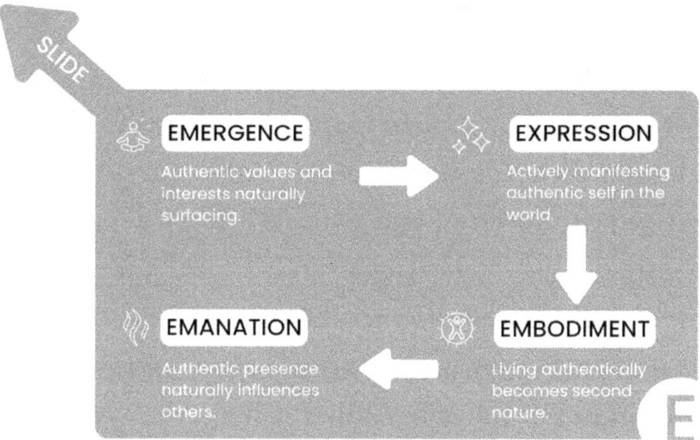

In Enlightenment, you'll progress through stages of organic **Emergence**, deliberate **Expression**, complete **Embodiment**, and natural **Emanation**. This progression represents the development of authentic selfhood and the gradual integration of genuine values into all aspects of life. The most important point here is that you will begin to live from your authentic center.

While the Enlightenment Quadrant is awesome, it is also truly energizing. It's joyful. It's life-affirming. It's the first time in a long time that you hold the reins. When I entered Emergence, I felt freer than I'd been in a long time. For me, this emerging core was my entrepreneurial self. I was creating and building. Yes, some of that was scary—I couldn't know what would take off and what wouldn't—but I believed in what I was doing and in myself wholeheartedly. I knew I would see this process through no matter what it took because I wasn't climbing back on the Conveyor Belt.

I had neglected this authentic version of myself for basically my entire life, so part of Emergence involved learning the skills and building the knowledge base I needed to create a business. Even though my undergrad degree was in business with a finance focus, working in someone else's established organization was totally different from starting my own. I had to go back to the beginning and think about what I wanted to create.

When I started taking the steps to bring that business to life, I moved into Expression. As an entrepreneur, that meant identifying myself as a business creator, joining organizations where I could network and meet other entrepreneurs, and working to promote and build my business—in other words, the externally visible things I was doing.

On the personal side, I was making conscious decisions when it came to my family and friends. I knew I wanted more time with my family, and I wanted to provide meaningful experiences and have heartfelt connections with Abby and my kids. So Abby and I started having weekly date nights, and I made sure I had one-on-one time with each of the kids doing something they loved, even if I wasn't completely sure I'd like it. It wasn't about me.

At some point, I moved from Expression to Embodiment, or the stage of being my authentic self without conscious effort. That shift was subtle, and I honestly can't remember when it happened. One day I was learning to listen to my inner voice, and the next day I was unconsciously understanding and living from that guidance. It felt as if I'd always lived that way. My business was thriving. My direction and next steps seemed crystal clear. I continued to grow, learn, and chase my interests. I questioned myself less, and I just *was*. Everything felt good—for the most part.

While Deconstruction was a difficult internal transformation, Enlightenment can be a difficult external transformation. Why? Because of relationships.

Whenever someone makes a change, no matter how trivial, it can elicit a negative reaction from others. They go on the defensive. They see you becoming somewhat of a different person, a much happier and more fulfilled person, and they start to question themselves. They may even go through a bit of Deconstruction. They see how effortlessly you can be yourself, they can tell that you're more confident, and they notice that stuff doesn't bother you as much anymore. But then they might wonder why the old you didn't seem good enough, and they ask if they are good enough for the new you. They also wonder why they can't seem to make the changes they want to make. They may get down on themselves for doing the same old thing all the time. So in an effort to feel better, they may cut you out.

Or maybe you've noticed that you just don't have as much in common with them because they're only interested in staying on the Conveyor Belt, but now you have new interests and things you want to do in your life. So you drift apart.

Either way, it's painful and unfortunately somewhat inevitable at this point.

But here's the hope. Maybe after some time apart, as you continue on into the Impact Quadrant, your friend, family member, or acquaintance will start to get real with themselves and decide they want to follow you in their own way. Someday you may come back together, both living awesome, full, authentic lives, all because *you* had the courage to walk this path.

And that's Emanation. Your authenticity radiates from you through everything you do. It inspires and attracts. How could it not? People may start asking for your advice or opinion. You may find new friends without much effort. You may see small changes in other people's lives or how the group dynamics shift when you're around. You may have more gravitas in places where you previously felt overlooked. I remember that people began asking for my opinion on business deals they were considering or seeking advice about how to do certain things. But the best part was finding groups of like-minded people with whom I could connect quickly and on a deep level because we were all living from our core.

The Enlightenment Quadrant requires both receptivity and courage as you learn to recognize, trust, and express your authentic nature in a world that may not immediately understand or support it. But that is when you establish the foundation for the meaningful fulfillment and contribution of the next and final quadrant.

EMERGENCE: LIVE FROM YOUR CORE VALUES

Emergence represents the organic surfacing of authentic elements after the clearing ground of Deconstruction. Unlike the open-ended Discovering period, you're now seeing and experiencing the actual formation and manifestation of genuine values, interests, and ways of being. This stage transforms possibilities into tangible realities. Where Discovering identified potential paths and ways of being, Emergence represents the natural formation of authentic patterns that arise from within rather than being consciously constructed. These traits and values were always there; they didn't need to be created in any way.

In this first stage of Enlightenment, you're building the foundation upon which all future authentic development builds. You're recognizing and acknowledging your inherent identity and purpose. You'll find that you have growing clarity about what truly resonates at a core level. You might see recurring themes in your interests (you're Kevin Costner again, and you love baseball, so go through your old baseball cards once a month and watch and listen to old games) or identify values that consistently guide your natural responses. You might feel like "Yes, this is truly me" more often. *Follow the yes*.

Arguably the best part of this stage is your growing sense of internal coherence and direction. I felt like I was coming back together after having been broken into pieces for years.

I felt at peace with the choices I made. However, there were still times when I inevitably slipped into an old conditioned pattern. As I was discovering my gifts and desires, I kept slipping back into Conforming patterns and trying to run my businesses how everyone else was running theirs. That often led to me becoming disengaged and the business failing. Pivot to the next one. As I gradually worked through Enlightenment and became more strongly connected with myself, the slips were smaller, more infrequent, and easy to dispel like an old thought pattern popping back into my head that caused me to doubt what I was doing, which would quickly counter with a different thought.

Just remember to have patience with yourself and trust in the organic process of authentic formation. You will get there, but maybe not as fast as you would like.

At this point, you'll find that you have a deeper relationship with yourself and your experiences such as a more observant, receptive relationship with your inner life, and you'll learn to notice and nurture authentic elements as they form. This process can lead to both increased self-trust and the challenge of protecting these emerging elements from premature exposure or external judgment before they've fully formed. In hindsight, you realize that you should have kept your baseball diamond a secret until it was completely built.

To move through this stage effectively, you have to balance receptivity with discernment by creating conditions that support authentic Emergence while developing the ability to recognize what is truly authentic versus what might be remnants of conditioning. That comes down to cultivating clarity about what genuinely resonates with you at a core level.

Think about researcher and author Brené Brown. During the period following her breakdown and spiritual awakening around 2007, she began recognizing authentic values and ways of being that were emerging naturally after she questioned her previous patterns. Moving beyond the exploration of vulnerability research, she began noticing consistent themes emerging in her own authentic responses to life. That highlights the two key points of Emergence: recognizing rather than constructing authentic elements and being open to those authentic elements through receptivity. Your genuine core values and authentic self are already inside you if you create space for them.

Like the first green shoots appearing after a forest fire, Emergence involves the recognition and nurturing of naturally arising authentic elements to form a genuine sense of self and purpose after questioning and dismantling inherited patterns. You're a phoenix rising from the ashes or a *Super Saiyan* [insert your name here] transforming.

EXPRESSION: SHOW YOUR TRUE COLORS

Expression follows Emergence as the active manifestation of your authentic self, representing the deliberate externalization of emerging authentic values, interests, and ways of being. This stage transforms internal recognition into external reality. Where Emergence identifies authentic elements forming within, Expression brings those elements into the world through tangible actions, decisions, and creative outputs. As you express your authentic self, you also enter the crucial testing ground for emerging authenticity. You begin to actively embody your authentic self through visible choices and creations.

If you're not building a baseball diamond, you might start another creative project that aligns with your emerging purpose, make decisions that clearly reflect your authentic values, or develop relationships that honor your genuine needs and boundaries. Oftentimes you'll feel both vulnerability and liberation since expressing your authentic elements involves risk yet validation through the alignment of your inner truth and outer action. You're walking the bridge of inner authenticity and outer reality.

As you continue to express your authentic self through your actions and choices, you'll have increased clarity through active feedback such as concrete information about what truly resonates with you in practice. You must balance courage with discernment, developing both the confidence to give form to emerging authenticity and the wisdom to integrate practical learning without compromising core values.

Another challenge lies in maintaining authentic expression while navigating practical realities and relationships. You have to keep building that baseball diamond, even when the hecklers show up. You may have to renegotiate boundaries, change communication patterns, or seek new communities that support your authentic expression, which can lead to the formation of more aligned connections. Yet this may also disrupt relationships built on previous patterns of interaction—

your old self. Don't be surprised if this continues into the next stage of Enlightenment: Embodiment.

After periods of physical suffering and personal questioning, artist Frida Kahlo moved beyond conventional artistic traditions to authentically express her experience of pain, identity, and Mexican heritage. She began creating deeply personal works, an act that required courage to give external form to internal truth, especially when people criticized her style or talent. She embraced vulnerability and creative action to transform her authenticity into a tangible reality that she shared with others.

This is the crucial step in bringing authentic selfhood into tangible reality—you're moving between merely recognizing authentic elements and fully living them in daily life. Like an artist giving form to an inner vision, Expression involves the satisfaction of seeing internal truth take external form.

EMBODIMENT: BEING

Embodiment emerges as the full integration of authentic values and ways of being into daily living, the seamless incorporation of authentic elements into your natural way of being. By this point, the conscious changes and choices you made in Expression have been woven into the very fabric of your identity and behavior. It's all second nature now. The foundation laid during the last phase becomes the launching pad for Embodiment, and later Emanation. The gap between your inner truth and outer living has disappeared as your values and purpose guide your behavior automatically.

You may have noticed a subtle shift as your values began to naturally align with your actions across all life domains. You have probably found yourself making decisions consistently from your authentic center without deliberate effort, responding to challenges in ways that naturally reflect your values or experiencing a seamless flow between purpose and daily activities. That's pretty great after the sheer torture of Despair, right? There will be a profound sense of resilience, integrity, and ease as the internal struggle between your authentic self and your old conditioned patterns largely dissolves.

Often there is also a natural simplification of life as your decisions and actions flow more consistently from your integrated authentic core. While this brings greater peace and increased clarity, it also requires maintaining this integration even under stress or in challenging environments. However, much of the work renegotiating boundaries and relationships in Expression may help alleviate some of those external pressures. No matter—hold tight to your core values and look inward for guidance in new contexts.

As you move deeper into Embodiment, you may experience greater presence and engagement with each moment as the energy previously consumed by internal conflict becomes available for full participation in life. That leads to deeper satisfaction in ordinary experiences. And though it may seem like you've reached the best, highest, truest form of self (and in comparison to where you started, you sort of have), there's still room for growth. You are not done yet, which is a good thing. You're entering a time of embodying authenticity while remaining open to continued evolution and refinement as your values deepen and mature through ongoing life experience.

This is a wonderful, beautiful time in life, but even roses have thorns, and so does the Enlightenment Quadrant. When I finally reached this part of my journey, I encountered something I hadn't intended: the shift in social dynamics and relationships. Earlier in the chapter I spoke about this more generally, but as I embodied my authentic self more and more, suddenly my friends on the Conveyor Belt and I just didn't have a lot to talk about. They saw the rest of their lives every day as sitting down at desks owned by other people, working, going home, and getting up to do the exact same thing the next day. I saw my feet walking out the door, not always sure of where I might be swept off to. Sure, I kept up some of our usual banter, but I wasn't always invested anymore. Years later, one or two of those friends joined me on the path of self-discovery, but not everyone. And that's okay. I still wish them well, and I keep going.

This shift also affected my relationship with identity and business. I'd worked so hard to create this self-sustaining entity, and I cared about it so much that at first I was resistant. I thought I could be both the primary operator and CEO, no matter how large my companies grew. But that made me the weak link. That was because I wouldn't let my daily operations tasks shift to the highly qualified team I had put in place, as they naturally should have, and that held everything up. So I learned the hard way that the business had outgrown what I could do in a day—shoot! a week. This was both rewarding and frustrating—frustrating since I'm not always good at letting go and rewarding since I had made something that could support so many people and serve value to the market. Once I did move into the CEO role, though, it allowed me to do so much more for the business and myself. It was freeing to know that the business didn't *need* me. I could use my time for strategy, building partnerships, and other long-term and big-picture work.

I think about what Bruce Lee said: "Be water, my friend." Adapt and flow wherever you feel called to go. During his later development of Jeet Kune Do when he famously gave that advice, he was moving beyond the deliberate application of martial arts techniques and embodying the philosophy of adaptability and authenticity in both his fighting style and his approach to life. His experience demonstrates the integration of values and principles until they become a natural way of being that transcends conscious application into spontaneous expression.

Embodiment represents the crucial achievement of living authentically without effort or pretense. Like a dancer who no longer thinks about the steps but simply moves with natural grace, this stage involves the satisfaction of *being* rather than *doing* authenticity; it's the transformation of being that permeates all aspects of life.

EMANATION: THE UNINTENDED BUT WONDERFUL IMPACT OF YOUR JOURNEY

Emanation represents the natural radiation of embodied authenticity beyond the individual. That's a lot. I know. It's when all the good stuff that's been happening inside you and that you've unleashed into the world begins to influence others and your environment like a light naturally spreading from its source or a magnetic quality that draws people and opportunities to you without deliberate effort. This also makes it a natural transition toward the service orientation of the Impact Quadrant.

You might notice others seeking your perspective or presence; you may find yourself naturally inspiring others without trying to do so. Others might observe how your way of being creates subtle shifts in group dynamics and environments. That could bring a sense of expanded Impact coupled with humility as your authentic presence affects others without deliberate intention. Emanation emphasizes the natural overflow of authenticity beyond self.

This unintentional growth of your sphere of influence opens opportunities for connection and contribution. You may find yourself navigating more requests for involvement, guidance, or collaboration as others are drawn to you, making you feel a greater sense of responsibility or obligation. The difficulty here is discerning which connections and requests truly align with your authentic path. You can't say yes to everything, even though you may want to. Remember, balance openness with boundaries—generosity in sharing your authentic presence and wisdom to protect the space needed for your continued authentic living.

A great example of this transition is Jane Goodall as she moved from field researcher to conservation advocate. After decades of embodying her authentic connection with and respect for chimpanzees and their habitat, she found her presence and perspective naturally drawing attention and creating influence without deliberate effort. Still today it would be all too easy to take every opportunity that comes her way, but she holds true to her message and her core values, which helps her create boundaries and take the opportunities that align with her authentic self. In other words, she doesn't have a McDonald's burger named after her, but instead, she founded the Jane Goodall Institute and partners with and speaks at conservation organizations all around the world. Her life bridges personal embodiment and deliberate service to larger causes.

Like a fully bloomed flower naturally releasing its fragrance, Embodiment is the effortless extension of authentic being beyond individual boundaries and eventually extends to the deliberate contribution that characterizes the Impact Quadrant. Think about it like this: The more you grow, the bigger your impact. That's when you can serve others in bigger and better ways. That's where the true Impact of the final quadrant lies; it's the heart of ikigai.

BEYOND SELF

While the Deconstruction Quadrant is by far the most emotionally difficult quadrant to move through, the Enlightenment Quadrant is the most personally demanding. Why? Because you're transforming both on the inside and in your actions. You're making conscious choices to share your authentic values and live from your core, which is both scary and exhilarating at times.

When I decided to take the leap and live from my authentic self, which for me was becoming an entrepreneur, I was still working for someone else. I had a mortgage and family to support, and I didn't know how long it would take to build that first business. Every day I had my feet in both worlds—the Conveyor Belt and the authentic me. And it was tough. There were times when I wanted to just go back to the old patterns because they were easier. But good things happen when you keep moving forward, even when it's hard.

Brené Brown and Frida Kahlo embraced the challenge of living from their full, authentic selves and in doing so inspired others to see themselves for who they were and create lives of meaning. Bruce Lee showed us how to be adaptable to the process as we continue to transform in our lives. Jane Goodall demonstrated the essential skill of discernment that must come as our spheres of influence grow.

None of us knows what our lives will look like or what we'll be doing tomorrow, let alone five or ten years from now. But if you learn to live from your authentic self, if you allow that inner voice to guide your actions, if you lean into your courage and develop discernment and healthy boundaries, and if you flow like water—that's when you'll live your true purpose.

SPECIAL DYNAMIC: THE COMMON SLIDE

Before you head into the Checkpoint, I have to address the most dangerous setback you might face when you reach Emergence: the common slide.

In the last chapter, I probably seemed overly cautious about subtle conditioning, or those deep-seated programs you may not even realize exist. Here's why. As the term *common slide* suggests, this is a regression from Emergence back to Conformity. Why would someone choose to slide? There are any number of reasons, but mainly it's enticing to slip back into the "easy life" when things get hard, especially if we're facing a certain amount of resistance internally and externally.

If you're in the process of switching careers, going back to school to retrain, or starting a business, there will be tough times when nothing seems to go right. Maybe you had to skip a class to pick up the kids from school or missed a deadline for filing important paperwork to take care of a sick pet. When those times inevitably come, if your people (your family, your closest friends) say things like "Well, maybe this isn't the time" or "You tried your best . . . you might be able to contact your old boss and see about your job," or anything that offers a potential solution by moving backward or giving up, you're headed down a slippery slope.

When you are the most vulnerable, fear, doubt, or practical concerns will rear up like a hydra ready to strike you back onto the Conveyor Belt. What is most dangerous is the idea that the Conveyor Belt could offer you temporary relief while you still try to move into your authentic life via a side hustle.

This is tempting—oh, so tempting.

But here's what happens too often. You think, *Yeah, I could go back to [insert job you hated] just to get a paycheck. That would leave my evenings free for family things and time to get [insert authentic life passion] going while still getting paid and having benefits.*

So you regress. You willingly jump on the slide moving from authentic purpose back onto the Conveyor Belt. Maybe it's fine for a while. Maybe it's even nice having small talk by the water cooler and catching up with your old colleagues who never left.

"Look who's back!" they'll say. "Couldn't cut it out there in dreamland?" Maybe they won't be so snarky about it, but their questions might feel like that to you.

"No, we just needed a little more stability while I get [insert authentic life passion] going. You know how it is. But I'm still going to keep at it." Then you toss your empty paper cup into the trash can and run back to your cubicle.

Days, weeks, and months pass, but you haven't made significant strides on your authentic life. First, you had a big project at your job to finish. Then the kids had fall sports games and practices. Then came the holidays. But it's January again. You've got this!

Except everyone gets sick, and it drags on for weeks.

Suddenly it's spring with all the spring activities and planning for summer vacation, and you have another big project.

Here's the good news though. Someday the kids will be grown up and out of the house. Then you'll be able to go live your authentic life without worrying so much about everything else.

Right?

I'm not going to answer that because you know it's not true. There will always be hard times. There will always be obstacles. There will *never* be the perfect time to build an authentic life unless you take that time now.

At some point it won't be this hard. At some point, maybe sooner than you know, you will make it out of the obstacles, and everything will be as you hoped.

But that's only possible if you don't stop. It's only possible if you keep moving forward to live the life you were born to live.

The people living their dreams are the ones who didn't stop trying to make their dreams come true.

The temporary relief you might feel from sliding back into old conforming patterns is just that—temporary. Too quickly you'll remember why you left in the first place, except it's harder to push yourself out of the comfort of easy back into trudging through hard. But it won't be difficult forever.

And who ever said hard is bad? Who got to decide that we should want an easy life? Happiness only exists because we know sorrow, pain, and anger. And the fulfillment found in ikigai and beyond exists because we know what it feels like to live an inauthentic life.

Whenever you hit a rough patch in Emergence or at any point really, whenever you feel the urge to turn back, first ask yourself *why*. Why are you thinking of sliding backward?

There are two slides: a strategic slide (like the scenario described above) and a reactive slide. Here's what a strategic slide is:

✎ Conscious decision to temporarily maintain conformity

- ✎ Clear awareness of the compromise you're making

- ✎ Defined timeline or conditions for authentic expression

- ✎ Continued internal development during external conformity

- ✎ Preservation of connection to authentic elements

- ✎ Deliberate preparation for future expression

And here's a reactive slide:

- ✎ Panic-driven retreat from authenticity

- ✎ Initial relief embraced as validation of the choice

- ✎ No clear plan for eventual expression

- ✎ Rationalization of conformity as "realistic" or "mature"

- ✎ Surprise when relief transforms into deeper conflict

- ✎ Avoidance of situations that trigger authentic awareness

No matter the rationale for the slide, it won't fix whatever problem you're experiencing at this moment. In fact, it could do more than just set you back and not fix the problem; it could completely derail your progress.

Rather than climbing the ladder and willingly hopping on that long slide back to the Conveyor Belt, enlist the help of a trusted friend or mentor and find a solution to the current issue. It may not be perfect and it may not be exactly what you want, but obstacles are only a nuisance until you find a way through them. And you will find a way through them if you keep trying.

Checkpoint

Enlightenment feels like a dream after living on the Conveyor Belt and transforming through Deconstruction. But even there you might still find yourself falling back into old programming, especially when things don't always work out how you wanted them to. It's all too easy to question the point of the journey itself.

Knowing that you've cleared the most obvious programming out of your life, be careful of the more subtle conditioning that might hold you back from time to time. Take a moment now to think back on some of the decisions you made in the past week.

- What decision did you make and why?

- Did it come from your authentic self?

- Or did subtle conditioning you hadn't noticed before influence your choice?

Consider working in weekly checks for a while as you live deeper and deeper in Enlightenment. On the other hand, spend some time reflecting on the Emergence of your authentic self.

- Did you ever imagine living this wonderful life?

Celebrate how far you've come and the obstacles you've conquered to get here. It's not easy, and most people don't even attempt it. But you did. And now you're sharing gifts with the world.

Whenever you feel old programming creeping in, remember this feeling of triumph. Remember why you started down this path in the first place. You can be perfectly happy living in Enlightenment for the rest of your life. But if you're even remotely curious to know if better is even possible, keep reading.

Chapter 8

IMPACT: LIVING BEYOND SELF

In Chapter 4, I told you about the NLP conference I attended that changed my life, but I didn't give you the whole story. I didn't share my *aha!* moment with you. So let's walk it back a minute.

In 2023, my company's biggest client pulled out of a deal, and I was happy to watch everything burn. Yes, that's weird for an entrepreneur to say. I felt relieved more than anything else. But it made me question why I was there. If I was an entrepreneur and glad that my most lucrative business was failing, what did that mean? I should've been crushed, but I wasn't.

I kept thinking, *There must be something more for me. There's a different reason I'm here, some different purpose.* I just needed to explore what that was.

Those ideas led me down the rabbit hole of trying out many self-discovery tools, except nothing worked as I thought it would. Then I found myself at that NLP conference sitting in a cohort with people who knew their purpose, talking about how they were going to use NLP to help others. All the while I was thinking, *What's* my *purpose?*

One student in the class said their purpose was to help people heal through plant medicine. Someone else was an energy healer whose purpose was to help people heal from trauma. There was a chiropractor who said his purpose was to bring health and wellness to others. Everyone around me could articulate their purpose, but I couldn't. It was so frustrating.

Where is my articulation? Where's my purpose? If I knew what it was, I could just run toward it. I only know what isn't my purpose.

I knew that building businesses to make money was not my purpose. In fact, that's what made me realize I'd been operating without a purpose. Yes, I was good at building businesses. And I guess the world needed some of what I was doing because people bought my products and services.

But I didn't love it. It didn't light me up inside, but I did it for the longest time. Finding that light was motivation enough for me to keep searching. The only thing I could articulate was that I wanted to help people, and I had a sense of wanting to bring them with me on this journey of discovering our purpose.

Then something funny happened.

I don't remember where I was, but I was praying, and out loud, I said, "I just want to find my purpose, God, so I can help other people find their purpose." I heard the words come out of my mouth, and everything shifted. A weight lifted off my shoulders. I felt lighter.

It also felt like God, in His loving and benevolent way, smacked me on the back of the head and said, "I've been giving it to you this whole time, but you've been overthinking it."

Again, I responded out loud, "Is it really this easy? Is my purpose to help get people aligned in order to find their purpose?"

The answer? *Yes!*

The further answer? *Stop trying to make this all about you. It's not. Also, I've figured this out for you already. Just accept it and move on to the next step already.*

As soon as I allowed myself to receive this message, when I stopped trying so hard to find something more complicated, and when I took down the walls—walls that were my own making—that's when I aligned. And everything was so much easier after that.

After the NLP conference, I attended Lewis Howes's Summit of Greatness in 2024, found StoryBuilders, started writing a book, and began working with Brand Builders Group to get my message out there. That is how it starts—putting my thoughts into a book focused on helping people get aligned with their purpose. I'd been staring at it the whole time and still missed it for years. But now that I know my purpose, I won't stop running toward it. And that's what I want for you.

NLP explains all the programming and conditioning we go through since most of us are not nurtured and nourished in alignment with our purpose. So we have to go through a period of conforming and being separated from our purpose. And then we find who we are, which is what I want this book to do. I want it to help you find your purpose, your ikigai, and help you share it with the world. Welcome to the Impact Quadrant.

GOING BEYOND SELF

You are now entering the nebulous, undefined fulfillment space in the Impact Quadrant. Why is this nebulous and undefined? Because once you've moved through Enlightenment to the point where you're looking for bigger and better ways to serve others, there is no limit. You can grow your Impact as big as you can possibly imagine.

This is the point where authentic selfhood extends into measurable and immeasurable contributions to others and the world—measurable in the sense that you know how many people you are serving and immeasurable because Impact has a rippling effect. The people you directly serve will then serve others who will serve others, and so on. You can never know how far-reaching your impact will be, which is beautiful if you stop to think about it.

But Impact doesn't just happen. It's a strategic progression of expanding influence. With this expanding influence comes a profound satisfaction from seeing your authentic values generate ever-growing, tangible, positive outcomes.

If my language here feels very full, bordering on over the top, well, it should because the work you do in the Impact Quadrant has a deeply profound effect on those around you. While the first three quadrants were inward-focused, self-centered in the sense that you were finding yourself, this quadrant is outward-focused. We're more concerned about what we can do for the world than for ourselves.

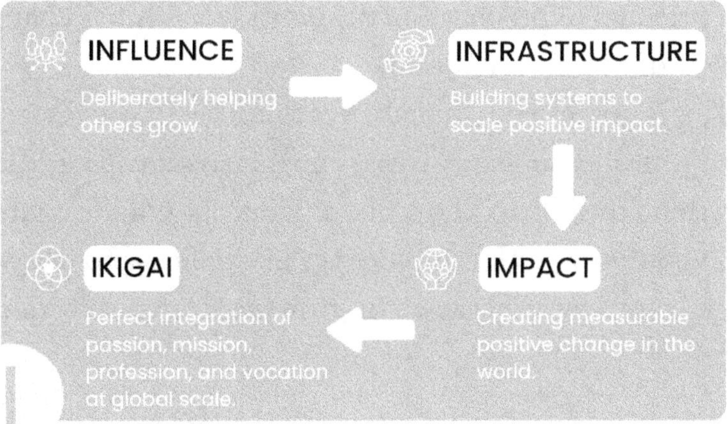

Throughout this quadrant, you will move through stages of deliberate **Influence** on others. You'll create sustainable **Infrastructure** to scale that Influence. That generates measurable and immeasurable **Impact** across populations. And ultimately, that leads to the complete integration of all **Ikigai** elements at the global scale.

True fulfillment emerges not from self-development alone but from the tangible manifestation of *authentic* selfhood through contribution to humanity. Your unique gifts have found their perfect expression in creating positive change that meets humanity's needs.

Understanding the Impact Quadrant explains both the path and the destination of authentic living. The journey begins by recognizing inherited patterns of living (Conveyor Belt Quadrant), progresses to questioning those inherited patterns (Deconstruction Quadrant), leading to developing through authentic self-realization (Enlightenment Quadrant), and naturally culminating in strategic contribution that creates both personal fulfillment and demonstrable positive change in the world (Impact Quadrant).

This is not the end, though. Reaching the Impact Quadrant doesn't mean you've grown as much as you can or learned everything there is to know about yourself. On the contrary, you'll continue to develop deeper as you expand outward. You'll enjoy the experience of growing in two directions at once.

INFLUENCE: HELPING OTHERS GROW

Influence represents the natural extension of authentic presence into deliberate impact on others. While Emanation is an *inadvertent* impact upon others, Influence is the *intentional* leveraging of authentic presence to inspire and effect positive change in those around you and your immediate community. This stage transforms your personal authenticity into a direct catalyst for growth in others, creating the foundation upon which all future impact builds.

As the first stage in the Impact Quadrant, Influence is characterized by the deliberate application of authentic presence to inspire, guide, and transform those within your immediate sphere. In practice, that might involve intentionally sharing insights to help others overcome challenges, consciously modeling authentic approaches that others can adopt, or deliberately guiding others through their own development journeys. Side effects may include a profound sense of purpose and effectiveness. While Emanation is spontaneous, Influence is deliberate.

Moreover, Influence significantly impacts how you now understand your purpose and potential. Your authentic gifts become clarified and refined through deliberate application since Influence provides feedback that reveals both areas of strength and those needing development. That can lead to a deeper understanding of your unique contribution and the challenge of distinguishing between effective influence and manipulation or control.

However, shifting from self-focused work to strategically applying your newly found authenticity to help others comes with its own set of challenges. You'll need to learn how to balance the responsibility and desire you feel to create deliberate Impact with respect for others' autonomy. That requires developing new capacities for discernment, ethical application, and balancing directed guidance with honoring others' journeys. The key is developing the wisdom to recognize when Influence should be withheld or redirected based on others' needs and readiness.

Thinking about it another way, it's like when you try something new that feels like it has changed your life, and you tell everyone in your life they should try it too. Some of them will also love it. Some of them will try it and not love it, and then they'll tell you about it. And some will give you a hundred reasons why they can't try it. Consider the *who* and the *what* and also what the other person needs before acting.

Following Brené Brown's viral TED Talk on vulnerability, she began deliberately applying her research and insights to help others develop courage and authenticity in their lives. Moving beyond simply sharing her findings, she started strategically designing experiences and content to influence how people understand and practice vulnerability. Her actions demonstrate how influence involves the intentional application of authentic wisdom and stories about her own journey to catalyze transformation in others who are ready to grow and change.

Influence represents the crucial beginning of intentional, authentic Impact beyond your individual development. You're the catalyst that enables transformation in others without controlling it. As part of the natural progression through this quadrant, once you've begun to extend your authentic presence into meaningful contribution to others' growth and development and have seen the positive change it has made in their lives, you'll want to scale your Impact. How? Through building the proper Infrastructure.

INFRASTRUCTURE: CREATING SYSTEMS TO SUPPORT EXPANSION

Infrastructure emerges as the deliberate creation of systems and structures that can sustain and scale authentic impact. That involves developing sustainable systems such as frameworks, methodologies, and platforms that can extend Impact beyond direct presence.

Where Influence creates direct impact through personal application—perhaps by being physically in the presence of others—Infrastructure creates the supporting structures through which authentic contribution can flow consistently and reach more people. Think building a website where people can access coaching programs, a blog, free videos on a social media channel dedicated to whatever you're doing, training others to implement your framework, or creating content and programs that can be licensed. No matter what you choose, take time to build systems that embody your authentic values.

This stage often brings a sense of expanding influence and responsibility as your contribution begins reaching people far beyond your immediate circles. It can also change how you relate to your authentic message. As you create systems, programs, content, or whatever it may be, you will find yourself refining and clarifying your core values to make them transferable across contexts. While you refine, you'll discover the universal elements of your message and the aspects that require adaptation for different audiences. That will lead to a deeper understanding of your essential message and the challenge of maintaining personal connection as Impact becomes more distributed. That is where growing deeper as you expand outward starts happening.

As you expand, be sure to maintain your integrity—stay true to your authentic self. You must develop the capacity to design scalable approaches with the wisdom to discern which aspects of authentic contribution can be extended broadly and which require more intimate contexts. Pay careful attention to how messages and methodologies translate across contexts.

A word of caution: This is where it's really easy to get caught up in the excitement and sometimes the hype of what you're doing. To build out some of these systems to scale, you may have to enlist the help of others because it can take specialized knowledge to create these systems well, manage your resources, and maintain integrity across multiple channels. There may be many new voices speaking into your contribution. Some of them may have good ideas that align with your values and desired transformation, and others won't. Hold true to your authentic center. Don't dilute your authentic values or lose connection with the human impact of your contribution for the sake of growth.

Also, give yourself the grace of time to do it well, not fast. You might be able to build a website overnight, but doing it thoughtfully, along with building out other systems and ideas, takes time. That's okay.

This book you're reading right now is an example of the Infrastructure phase, including the fact that I've enlisted the help of a team to bring my message to the page. Along with my book, I'm growing my social media content and continuing to refine my message for you, the person on this journey. I'm also building out a few more programs and ideas to help expand my reach. It takes time to create these systems and put them in place, but I know it's time well spent.

Consider Marie Kondo. As a child, she began tidying and organizing with her mother in their home. That led to Marie tidying her classroom at school and later founding her first tidying company while still at the university. As her work developed, she wrote her first book, developed a series of videos to spread her message, wrote even more books, made television appearances, and eventually landed on Netflix. All this was years in the making, one step at a time, growing her team, refining her message, and developing new ways to amplify her message and help an increasingly global audience "spark joy."

Additionally, from working directly with clients, she developed a clear methodology and communication approach that she expanded to reach millions worldwide, and in doing so, she learned how to translate her message across cultures and language barriers. She held true to her tidying-up framework even in light of pushback and mocking. And now with three small kids of her own, she has acknowledged that sometimes you have to be flexible with tidying. But no matter what, she has held true to her authentic self and values: intentional living and choices about what to bring into your life.

Infrastructure represents a crucial expansion of authentic impact beyond direct influence. From the satisfaction of seeing authentic values reach and influence many people through carefully designed channels, you learn how your individual contribution can change the world if you're willing to put in the work to expand through thoughtfully planned Infrastructures. As you amplify your authentic contribution, your positive impact grows, making the world better.

IMPACT: WIDENING YOUR SPHERE OF INFLUENCE

Impact represents the significant expansion of authentic contribution to create measurable positive change through the Infrastructure developed in the Infrastructure phase. To some extent, Infrastructure and Impact overlap and occur somewhat simultaneously. As you build and implement the support you need to grow, you'll begin to see the results of your widening influence.

Where Infrastructure created the supporting structures and delivery systems, Impact leverages those systems to generate substantial, measurable transformation across multiple contexts and populations. This stage focuses on the actual difference made in the world rather than just the reach of your message. I think of this as the manifestation of purpose through tangible outcomes.

As time goes on, you'll be able to measure and validate the real-world effects of your work through results that can be observed, measured, and refined for even greater effectiveness. That could look like leading movements that transform industries or communities, implementing programs that address significant needs across populations, or developing innovations that simultaneously solve significant problems for many people. You'll feel a profound sense of fulfillment and validation as you see your authentic purpose create meaningful difference at scale, transforming how you understand your contribution to the world.

You'll most likely develop a more nuanced understanding of how change actually happens and discover the power and limitations of your approach through direct evidence of its effects. You may also have a deeper confidence in your authentic contribution and the humility from recognizing the complex nature of meaningful change.

At the same time, there is also an immeasurable impact as the people you've helped transform do the same for their communities. This is the ripple effect of your authentic values and work, the more immaterial part of your Impact. It is impossible to know how many people will be helped by what you're doing. And to me, that makes it all the more important.

As with Infrastructure, the challenge of Impact is balancing the focus on measurable outcomes with continued fidelity to authentic values and purpose, and respecting the complexity of the systems being influenced. To do that well, you'll need to develop the capacity to measure and validate impact with the wisdom to recognize that not all meaningful outcomes can be immediately quantified or attributed.

However, from an organizational standpoint, creating sophisticated approaches to measuring effectiveness, gathering feedback, and continuously improving systems based on real-world impact will make your work better and better. So measure where you can. Don't be afraid to grow and adapt. Stay true to your authentic self.

Impact represents the fulfillment of authentic potential through tangible contribution and creating measurable positive change in alignment with your deepest values and unique gifts. That is how you move from building systems to validating their effectiveness through real-world transformation. As each of those parts becomes more integrated, fusing so you don't know where one ends and another begins, that's when you've entered Ikigai.

IKIGAI: LIVING AT THE CONVERGENCE OF PASSION, MISSION, PROFESSION, AND VOCATION

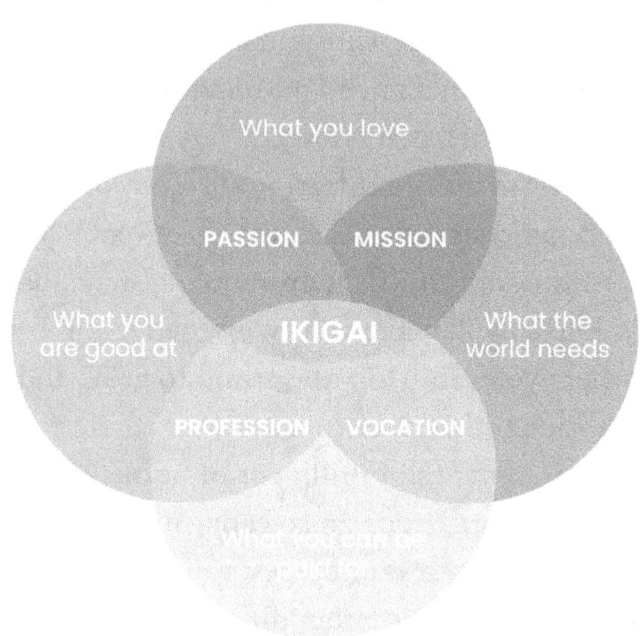

Ikigai is the culmination of authentic Impact characterized by the effortless flow between authentic being and worldwide service where your unique gifts find their perfect expression in meeting humanity's needs. Said another way, this stage transforms widespread impact into harmonious wholeness that serves humanity while fulfilling your purpose.

The measurable impact developed during the last phase now perfectly integrates with all aspects of meaningful purpose, creating a legacy that continues beyond an insdividual lifetime. That might look like finding your unique approach to creating positive change across cultural boundaries, discovering sustainable abundance flowing naturally from authentic contribution, or experiencing your deepest values resonate with universal human needs.

Once you reach Ikigai, you'll have a profound sense of rightness and completion as all dimensions of purpose align in service to individual fulfillment and collective well-being. You may feel a transformation in how you experience your relationship with humanity and purpose, moving beyond identification with personal achievement to experience yourself as a channel for something more significant and an expanded sense of possibility through that integration. That will give you more profound peace as well as the challenge of maintaining practical effectiveness while holding this transcendent perspective.

Once you reach Ikigai, you'll have to learn how to balance universal vision with practical implementation, which involves adapting to changing global needs. That requires developing the capacity to hold the complete vision of integrated purpose and the wisdom to express that vision through practical systems that create sustainable, positive change.

Let's look at a couple of things here. First, by this point, you will most likely have a team working with you to bring this vision to the world, bringing its unique challenges of working toward a goal for the greater good while also being a boss. And frankly, some days it will be hard to wear those different hats. Build in the time you need to rest and reconnect with your authentic vision. Seek mentors where and when you need them. Lead with heart and honesty. That won't make everything perfect, but it will certainly make it easier.

Second, this stage includes transcending the apparent contradictions between personal and collective good by discovering how authentic purpose naturally serves universal needs when fully expressed. There is an inherent connection between individual fulfillment and global contribution.

While this brings unprecedented wholeness and peace, it also requires maintaining this integration amid the complexities of global systems and diverse cultural contexts. The struggle lies in sustaining the delicate balance of all Ikigai elements while navigating the inevitable tensions of worldwide impact.

If all this seems quite complex, it should. Ikigai is intentionally a challenge, a call to action, a see-how-far-you-can-go situation. Not everyone will reach Ikigai, and not everyone wants to. You can be perfectly happy in the Enlightenment Quadrant, and that's perfectly fine.

But I've found that once you reach Enlightenment, once you see how changing your life positively affects those around you, you're filled with a natural desire to do more. Once someone tells you how your actions helped them do x, y, and z, you will want to help more people. You can step off the path at any point and make your home, but at least for me, I want to see how many people I can help.

Enter Hayao Miyazaki. Throughout his career, his passion for storytelling and animation (what he loves), his mastery of filmmaking and artistic vision (what he's good at), his successful Studio Ghibli productions (what creates sustainable livelihood), and his environmental and humanistic messages (what the world needs) achieved perfect integration on a worldwide scale. Moving beyond separate aspects of his work, he experienced the complete fusion of personal purpose with global impact through films such as *Princess Mononoke* and *Spirited Away* that both carry profound environmental and spiritual messages to audiences across cultures and generations. Miyazaki's life illustrates how Ikigai involves the seamless integration of all Ikigai elements at a global scale, demonstrating how personal, authentic purpose can achieve perfect alignment with worldwide service to create a life of unprecedented meaning and impact.

Ikigai represents the ultimate expression of authentic purpose in service to humanity. Like a master symphony where every element works perfectly to create transcendent beauty, this stage involves the profound satisfaction of experiencing complete alignment between authentic gifts and global contribution through one seamless expression.

THE LONG AND WINDING ROAD

The Impact Quadrant is both exhilarating and terrifying. It's exhilarating in the sense that you're experiencing many positive effects of living your authentic purpose. It's terrifying in the sense that you're putting your message out in the world where other people will experience it wherever they are and have opinions about it.

As mentioned earlier in Infrastructure, you can't dilute your message to serve everyone. In trying to serve everyone, you serve no one. So if someone responds negatively to your message, maybe it's not for them. Or perhaps it is, but they're not ready to receive it yet. Either way, stay true to you.

That being said, even when you reach Ikigai, you will continue to grow and change. While you may have started out living your authentic purpose one way and saying one thing, that doesn't mean you won't want to do something different at some point. Your values and purpose won't change, but the way they manifest in your life might. You'll see this all the time.

It's the young person who starts their career teaching but after a decade or two pivots to something new such as becoming a travel agent. They're no longer in a school setting, but they are certainly still teaching—this time teaching others about different cultures through helping people travel and create memorable experiences.

Maybe it's the entrepreneur who starts out creating businesses focused on serving a market need and making capital and then pivots to creating a space where people can learn about themselves and grow. Or maybe it's something more subtle like a plastic surgeon working for high-profile clients and pivoting into medical missions work where they help kids with cleft palates. Once you've found your authentic purpose, it will always be there guiding your choices. But don't think for one second that you have to stay locked into what you're doing right now for the rest of your life.

I'm still early in my Impact Quadrant journey and loving every minute of it. As I continue to build out Infrastructure and find ways to help people navigate this journey and facilitate their own way through the framework, I take every day one step at a time, doing the next right thing that feels aligned with my purpose of helping others find and live in their purpose.

As long as you've navigated the path and discovered your authentic values—as long as you live in alignment with your authentic purpose—you can never go wrong.

 Checkpoint

The world is waiting for you!

As you travel through the Impact Quadrant, you may find yourself in each subquadrant all at once. After all, you may be working on building an infrastructure for your business or building your impact while contributing your time to various organizations and groups that expand your influence. But because you've worked so hard to get to this point, I would suspect that you haven't taken much time to celebrate the self-work you've done to get here, the hard decisions you had to make, the changes you implemented, and everything you've accomplished along the way. So put down your phone, close your email, and grab a pen and a piece of paper (yes, a physical pen and a physical piece of paper), and let's take a moment to reflect on your journey.

Think back to the start of this process, what your life was like, and how it felt. Sit with that for a moment. Next, think about where you are now, about everything that had to change for you to be here in the Impact Quadrant. With that in mind, write your answers to the following questions:

What was the calling that set you on the Path of Purpose, and why did you choose to answer it? Or what was the disconnect in your life that set you on the Path of Purpose, and why did you choose to connect with your authentic self?

- ✎ If you had to pick one pivotal moment from each quadrant, what would they be?

    - ○ What did you learn from those moments?

    - ○ How did they propel you forward?

    - ○ If you could thank each of those younger versions of yourself, what would you say?

- ✎ What has been the best part of your journey through the Path of Purpose?

- ✎ How have you been able to positively impact those around you?

- ✎ And because the work is never done, *what is next for you?* What is the biggest goal or dream you can imagine?

- ✎ How could you change the world if you accomplished that goal or dream? How many lives could you touch?

Life moves fast. If you don't take time to reflect, it's easy to forget your accomplishments and take it all for granted. So as you move forward, take time to refocus on *why* you're doing what you're doing and celebrate how far you've come.

Chapter 9

TAKE THE NEXT STEP

The spotlights from the back of the auditorium highlight the stage as the crowd in the audience settles in and quiets down. I'm standing in the wings, eyes closed in a silent prayer of thanksgiving because the moment I've been waiting for has finally arrived.

Peeking out through the curtains, I see Abby and my kids front and center. The rest of my family fills the first row. I adjust the cordless mic I'm wearing as my stage manager counts me down. My intro plays, I take a deep breath, and I step out into the lights with a huge smile on my face.

Everyone starts clapping and cheering. And they're clapping for me. I'm guessing most of them have read the book or attended one of my seminars, and they're excited. They're inspired. Many of them have already started the work to change their own lives, moving the needle in the direction of their happiness and purpose.

I can't stop beaming. I feel a deep satisfaction and actualization as I see people I've been able to help live the lives they were always meant to live. Their fulfillment is my fulfillment. Along with the emotional wholeness, I'm physically in shape and feeling great. And I'm proud of myself for accomplishing what I set out to do: help people find and live their purpose.

As the music fades, the clapping subsides, and I begin to speak.

No matter where you are in life, you can always become the prime version of yourself, the person living your purpose. You are one decision away from completely changing your life, and that decision can be made at any given moment. But that's always one decision we put off. Why? Because we're caught up in our programming.

Programming is the messaging and habits instilled in us our entire lives, either directly through things we've been taught, indirectly through what we see and hear others do, or what's been made desirable. It's an externally imposed version of who people expect us to be. This isn't all bad; hopefully, we've learned good habits such as eating our vegetables, getting our work done on time, and being a productive member of society. However, when those programs override our inborn values or desires, when they no longer serve us and yet we can't seem to escape them, that's when problems arise.

That's when you know you're stuck on the Conveyor Belt.

To break free and discover your authentic self and your authentic purpose, you have to jump the belt. That's the first step on your journey of the Path of Purpose.

When you picked up this book, I imagine you were near the end of the Conveyor Belt at the Conflicted subquadrant. You knew something was wrong, but maybe you didn't know why, and maybe you didn't know what to do with those feelings. As you read about Deconstruction, you may have been inspired to explore what was in your heart. You may have decided that you wanted to see what else life had to offer and discover what desire had been buried in your heart. At this point, you might already be in Enlightenment, taking the steps you need to set up a new way of living.

Or maybe you've read through this like a novel and decided it's too hard, that it's just not for people like you.

Here's why that's wrong and why you should want to put in the work to live your purpose out loud. If you don't follow the Path of Purpose, if you don't discover the purpose buried in your heart, if you don't go after your ikigai, you're depriving yourself and those around you of the best, happiest, and most fulfilled version of you. You're dismissing and withholding the unique gifts you've been given. You're wasting your opportunity to improve your life and the lives of those around you.

You deserve more. You deserve better.

Your family and friends deserve more.

The world needs you—yes, *you* specifically and what you have to offer.

I understand that what I'm saying and what I'm asking you to do may be a lot. I know it can be scary because I've been through it and have come out the other side a happier, satisfied, fulfilled person. And you will too.

If you're still holding back, it could be because you've not reached the breaking point yet, and maybe you, like me, need to hit that rock bottom. But you don't have to. It all depends on what I call the Misalignment Ratio and the Action Threshold. The Misalignment Ratio is the sum of your authentic desires divided by the impact of your limiting programming.

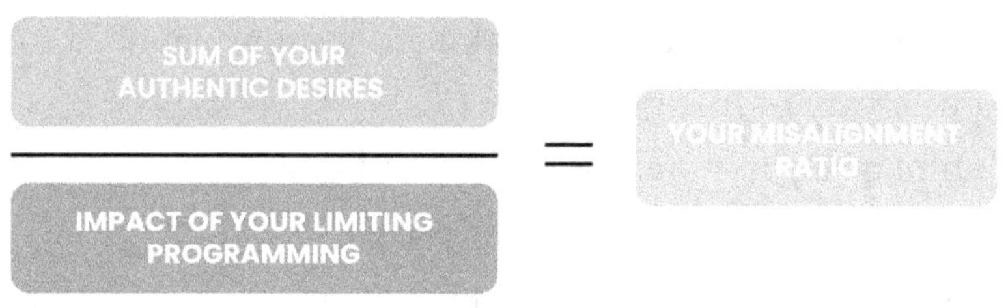

This ratio creates a beautiful tension in your life right around the moment you enter the Conflicted subquadrant. As the programming running your life begins to fail you more and more, and it will, the impact of your limiting programming grows, crushing your authentic desires, and that is when the real pain starts.

That's the feeling of living an increasingly smaller life. That's when the things you're doing just have no meaning because you feel like you're not significantly contributing in ways that suit you best. You may feel disconnected from yourself or like you're watching your life from the outside. Then, when you talk to people about your feelings, they say, "Meh, that's normal. I'm miserable too."

This is the crossroads.

Massive action is only taken when your Misalignment Ratio is greater than your Action Threshold. That's when the pain of staying the same is greater than the pain of change. That's when you will change. And you will take massive action at some point or another.

Some people have lower thresholds and make changes sooner. Others have higher thresholds and endure in misalignment for years. But the most powerful approach isn't waiting for your threshold to be crossed. It's about consciously lowering your threshold through increased self-awareness and making the changes you need to make sooner.

That's why I wrote this book. I want to help you become more self-aware so you can take action to make change.

Before you ask, there's no assessment to measure your authentic desires and the impact of your limiting programming. I can't tell you what quadrant and subquadrant you're in. These aren't quantifiable things. They're feelings. You already know you have things you really want to do that just feel good in your soul. You also know there are things (excuses, people, emotions) you are allowing to hold you back from doing the things that feel good in your soul, some of them unconscious and some known. And yes, I said *you* are allowing yourself to hold you back *because you have the choice to do something different.*

When you make that choice to take action, it will probably be somewhat difficult, but change isn't supposed to be easy. That's what makes it transformative. But it is absolutely one hundred percent worth it.

Remember in Chapter 4 when I talked about *Dragon Ball Z*? You have the chance right now to choose to become the *Super Saiyan* version of yourself—the best, most fulfilled, positive influence on the world.

Take a moment and imagine what that looks like. You read my *Super Saiyan* vision at the start of this chapter. I'm speaking from a stage to thousands of people, coaching tens of thousands more through the infrastructures I've set up, and making the world better by helping others live their purpose.

So what is it for you? What does your best life look like? Read the questions below and then close your eyes and visualize yourself there, including smells, physical sensations, everything. Get specific.

Where are you and what are you doing?

Are you at a desk running your business? If so, what is your business?

Or are you helping others directly? Is it one-on-one or in groups? Is it through a nonprofit or a mission?

Who is with you or around you? How do you feel physically and emotionally?

If you were able to visualize this future best life clearly and really feel the emotions that go along with it, that's awesome. Hold those feelings and ideas in your heart.

If it was harder for you to paint that picture and feel those feelings, that's okay too. I'm here to help you find that vision.

Deep down, you already know what's next.

So take the first step. Then take another. You're not starting from scratch. You're starting from truth.

Ready?

Let's go!

ACKNOWLEDGMENTS

Abby, none of this happens without you. The late nights, the uncertainty, the moments when I had to completely fall apart to rebuild myself. You gave me space to question everything and love to come home to. That's everything. YOU'RE everything.

To Olivia, Charlie, Jack, Luke, and Wendy: You five are my greatest teachers and my reason for living.

And Lucy, thanks for the snuggles. You're a good dog.

Mom, you gave me roots strong enough to weather any storm. To Jette, Emily, and Eric, watching each of you navigate your own paths has taught me more than you know. Dad, I wish you were here to see this.

To every member of "the gang." There are still large swaths of me that would trade it all for those endless summers we used to have growing up.

To all my mentors who saw something in me before I could see it in myself. You challenged me, supported me, and refused to let me play small.

To the friends and family who believed in this project when it was just scattered ideas and big dreams, you know who you are. I couldn't possibly name everyone, but your impact is woven into these pages. When's the next game night?

To Jen, Erin, Bill, and the team at StoryBuilders for being a fantastic publishing partner.

To Jay, Isla, and the team at Brand Builders for tirelessly keeping me on track and my eye on the prize.

To Aman, James, Myka, and the Viral Slice crew for making me look good in front of the world, and for being an indispensable partner in getting my message out there.

And finally, to shooting stars, fantasy books, disc golf, temples, physics, Jason Mraz, every gym I've ever sweated in, the love of learning, insatiable curiosity, and of course, camels.

I love you all and always will.

Thank you all for being part of this journey.

NOTES

1   "Checkered Game of Life," National Museum of American History, Behring Center, Smithsonian Institution, http://bit.ly/3VIJ6bH..

2   Donetta Allen, and Pat Riso, "The Game of Life Celebrates 50 Years," Hasbro, February 12, 2010, https://corp.hasbro.com/news-releases/news-release-details/game-life-celebrates-50-years.

3   Ralph Waldo Emerson, Essays: First Series, 1841 (Project Gutenberg, 2001), https://www.gutenberg.org/cache/epub/2944/pg2944-images.html#link2H_4_0002.

4   Ralph Waldo Emerson, *The Divinity School Address* (London: Philip Green, 1903), 68.

ABOUT THE AUTHOR

Eli Bowman is an author, in-demand keynote speaker, coach, and seven-figure entrepreneur who helps people bridge the gap between their current reality and their dream life. He is the creator of the groundbreaking Path of Purpose© framework, which guides individuals through the transformational journey from unconscious living to authentic impact.

After hitting rock bottom through self-destructive decisions driven by negative mental programming, Eli transformed his life by identifying and uninstalling the limiting beliefs that had been running his operating system his entire life. He bootstrapped a startup to a multi-million dollar valuation with over forty employees, only to discover that business achievements alone lacked true purpose. This realization led him to his real calling: guiding others to identify and remove what blocks their path to fulfillment.

As a neuro-linguistic programming (NLP) Master Practitioner, Eli creates powerful breakthrough moments for individuals and audiences by revealing fascinating insights about the brain and the unconscious mind. His work focuses on helping people distinguish between borrowed values and authentic purpose, reprogram their mental loops from mediocrity to excellence, and align their daily lives with what genuinely matters to them.

Eli lives with his wife Abby, their five children (Olivia, Charlie, Jack, Luke, and Wendy), and their dog Lucy. When he's not writing or speaking, you can find him playing disc golf, traveling, and making unforgettable memories with his family and friends.

For more information, visit www.elibowman.com or connect with Eli on Instagram: @eli.bowman